Lou Kriscoe

Books by Burt Hochberg

TITLE CHESS
WINNING WITH CHESS PSYCHOLOGY, with Pal Benko

POWER CHESS

GREAT GRANDMASTER BATTLES FROM RUSSIA

POWER CHESS

GREAT GRANDMASTER BATTLES FROM RUSSIA

Paul Keres

International Grandmaster

**Edited by
Burt Hochberg**

DAVID McKAY
COMPANY, INC.

Designed by M 'N O Production Services, Inc.

Chess diagrams by M-Mate-Chess

Library of Congress Cataloging-in-Publication Data

Keres, Paul
     Power chess : great grandmaster battles from Russia / Paul
Keres : edited by Burt Hochberg. — 1st ed.
          p.   cm.
     Collection of twenty-two columns written by Paul Keres for
Chess life magazine from 1968 to 1975.
     Includes index.
     ISBN 0-812-91949-1
     1. Chess—Tournaments—Soviet Union.   2. Chess—Collections of games.   I. Hochberg, Burt.   II. Chess life.   III.
Title.
GV1455.K43   1991
794.1'57—dc20   91–17909

Manufactured in the United States of America

98765432

First Edition

CONTENTS

PART III
ENDGAMES UNDER THE MICROSCOPE

INTRODUCTION

In Estonia almost everyone plays chess, and the family into which Paul Keres was born in 1916 provided him with two early opponents: his father and his brother. It soon became clear that Paul was no ordinary player, and by the time he had reached his teens his household rivals could no longer offer him an interesting challenge. Neither could anyone else in his hometown. Casting his nets farther afield, he began playing games by mail, and within a short time he was playing hundreds of them.

In correspondence chess, which is played at the rate of one move every few days, a player can attempt sacrificial combinations he wouldn't dare try over the board, since with plenty of time for analysis he can eliminate the possibility of overlooking a tactical refutation. But one can analyze only so far; an unsound combination is no less unsound simply because analysis has failed to reveal some tiny crack in its foundation.

Since young Paul Keres was inordinately fond of sacrificing pieces, he was forced to calculate deeply and as accurately as possible. Although he sometimes paid a price for attacking too passionately and overstepping the bounds of reasonable risk, the analytical skills he acquired proved much more valuable, and they helped make him one of the immortals of chess.

And they were instruments in making him one of the immortal chess writers. Although all grandmasters know what to do with their pawns and pieces, very few indeed feel at all comfortable when asked to explain how they work their magic.

Keres had the rare ability to make grandmaster chess comprehensible. In his annotations he explained how this move, by weakening a critical square, drags behind it a whole chain of consequences; why an attractive alternate line of play fails to meet the logical needs of the position; why now, not before or later, is the right moment to switch to the endgame. A game annotated by Keres is like an adventure story in which the connections between all the characters and all the events can be clearly seen and understood.

In 1967, shortly after being appointed editor of *Chess Life* magazine, I invited Keres to become a regular contributor. I greatly admired his collection of his own best games, and I wanted him to analyze current tournament games in a similar manner. He agreed at once, but to avoid the possibility of poaching on the territory of American players who might wish to analyze their own games for *Chess Life,* he proposed limiting himself to games played by Soviet grandmasters.

Keres thus became the first Soviet grandmaster to conduct a regular column in an American chess magazine. His first article appeared in January 1968, and from then until his shockingly premature death in 1975 he sent me more than forty articles.

Here are some of the most dramatic and instructive chess struggles between the best players of modern times—incredible rook sacrifices by Bronstein, inspired kingside attacks by Tal and Spassky, heroic defenses by Korchnoi, subtle endgames by Petrosian and Karpov, positional masterpieces by Keres himself.

In his *Chess Life* articles Keres returned repeatedly to several favorite themes. Although he strongly advocated opening preparation at home, he also warned of its dangers. He emphasized that real chess accomplishment was impossible without a deep understanding of the endgame. And he railed against the growing lack of fighting spirit in modern tournaments.

In a long letter to me in response to a few questions I had asked him soon after his first *Chess Life* article appeared, he delivered himself of some strong opinions on the latter subject. Following are edited excerpts from that letter, dated February 2, 1968:

> I have always been critical of the half-point tactics, as you call it, in tournament chess. But I cannot fully blame the players. In my opinion, the first step in this wrong direction was taken by FIDE, and it is continuing.
>
> Take all the tournaments in the World Championship series, for instance. It is good, of course, that these tournaments include players from all over the world, but the target of these tournaments should not be the world championship. Most of the players in the preliminaries have nothing to do with that title but play only for further qualification, not just for first place but for the first *n* places. The creative side of the game doesn't matter; only the point is king.
>
> Since the participants are of uneven strength, the leading grandmasters use simple arithmetic to plan where to get the needed points. Of course it is not reasonable to take risks against a leading rival; it is easier to obtain points from the weaker opponents. Only if the arithmetic does not go according to plan may it become necessary to "bite" a rival.

In my opinion, tournaments like this will lead to the death of creative chess, the kind of chess which millions of chess fans like so much and which was the reason every one of us started to play chess in the first place. . . .

For this book I have selected the cream of Keres's forty *Chess Life* articles—twenty-two in all. I have edited them anew, retitled them, converted the notation to algebraic where necessary, added new diagrams, and grouped the articles in logical categories.

This book would not have been possible without the cheerful cooperation of Al Lawrence, Executive Director of the U.S. Chess Federation. I owe a debt of gratitude to my good friend Bruce Pandolfini, a great chess author in his own right, who encouraged me to undertake this project. And I am grateful to copy editor Tom Tucker for so mercilessly exposing my notational and diagrammatical inaccuracies.

And once again I thank my good wife, Carol, for aid and comfort beyond the call of duty.

Burt Hochberg
January 1991

KINGSIDE CRUSHES

PART I

PETROSIAN IN TAL'S CLOTHING

**Petrosian vs. Estrin; English Opening
Moscow Championship, 1968**

This year's Moscow Championship was a fine, strong competition with eight grandmasters, including World Champion Tigran Petrosian. The public was particularly interested in his games, since he would soon be defending his title against Korchnoi or Spassky.

Petrosian played solid positional chess, generally without brilliant effects, and this enabled him to tie for first place without a single loss in fifteen games. This was his second tournament in a row (Bamberg was the first) in which he did not lose a game—something for his challenger to think about!

Petrosian's strictly positional approach has come under criticism recently, but the following short game demonstrates that he can play very aggressively when the need arises.

White: Tigran Petrosian
Black: Yakov Estrin

English Opening

1	c4	e5
2	g3	Nc6
3	Bg2	d6
4	Nc3	Be6

This makes no sense here. Better is 4 . . . g6 at once.

5	d3	g6
6	b4!	

As a consequence of Black's inaccurate fourth move, White can make this important advance without further preparation.

6 . . .		Qd7
7	b5	Nd8
8	Nf3	Bg7

Estrin's opening play is far from good. He should play 8 . . . Bh6, taking care of the threat 9 Ng5 and exchanging his opponent's strong bishop.

9	Ng5	e4

This move, too, must be criticized. Since White is better developed, the further opening of the position benefits only him. Therefore, 9 . . . Nf6 is preferable.

10	Bb2	exd3
11	Qxd3	a6
12	h4!	

As we can see, the world champion can play very sharply and aggressively given the right circumstances. This is much stronger than a good positional move like 12 0-0 or 12 a4.

Black has difficult problems. His king will be unsafe on either wing, and he will have trouble along the a1-h8 diagonal, which he so carelessly opened on his ninth move.

12 ...	axb5
13 cxb5	Ne7

Certainly Black would prefer 13 ... Nf6 were it not for the strong reply 14 Nce4!. On 14 ... Qe7, White could get the idea of sacrificing his queen with 15 Qd4 Nh5 16 Qxg7! Nxg7 17 Bxg7 with the terrible threat of 18 Nf6 + .

14 Qd2	0-0

Castling is very dangerous, but there's not much else Black can do about the threat of 15 Nce4. White can carry out that threat even on 14 ... h6, though 15 Nxe6 would also be strong.

15 h5	gxh5
16 Rxh5	

White has no need to rush his attack. After 16 Nxh7 Kxh7 17 Rxh5 + Kg8 18 Ne4 or 18 Nd5 Black still has the defense 18 ... f6.

16 ...	Bf5
17 Be4	Bg6

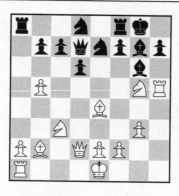

18 Rxh7!

This exchange sacrifice is decisive, robbing the black king of its last defense.

        18 ...   Bxh7
        19 Bxh7+   Kh8
        20 0-0-0

Now there is no adequate defense against 21 Rh1. An amusing finish would be 20 ... Bxc3 21 Qxc3+ f6 22 Qxf6+!, but Estrin prefers another way to go down.

        20 ...   Ng8
        21 Rh1   Nh6
        22 Nd5   f6

Black has nothing but forced moves. This is the only way to protect the knight.

23 Ne4

Also possible is 23 Nf4 fxg5 24 Rxh6, threatening both 25 Ng6 mate and 25 Bf5+ winning the queen. At this point there are many ways to win.

        23 ...   Rxa2

On 23 ... Kxh7 24 Nexf6+ wins easily.

24 Rxh6!	Bxh6
25 Qxh6	Qg7
26 Qh4!	Black resigned

Further resistance is hopeless. For instance, 26 ... Qxh7 27 Bxf6+ Rxf6 28 Qxf6+ Qg7 29 Qxd8+, or 26 ... Rxb2 27 Bg6+ Kg8 28 Nexf6+ Rxf6 29 Nxf6+ Kf8 30 Nh7+, etc.

(*October 1968*)

FORCED SACRIFICE

Keres vs. Lutikov; Ruy Lopez
Pärnu 1971

The Estonian town of Pärnu, a holiday resort on the Baltic Sea, has a fairly long chess tradition. Next to Tallinn it is the most important chess center in Estonia, and in 1936 it had the privilege of issuing the first Estonian chess magazine.

Pärnu has played a significant role in my chess development. While living there I played in my first chess tournament (in 1929) and conducted hundreds of correspondence games, and it was there that I grew to maturity and won the championship of Estonia in 1935.

The town also boasts one of the oldest chess clubs in Estonia. Founded in 1896, the club celebrated its 75th anniversary in 1971, an occasion that called for a jubilee tournament with grandmaster participation.

Of course it was a pleasure for me to play there

again after a long absence, and the organizers also were able to attract grandmasters Stein, Bronstein, Tal, and Lutikov. The result was a fine tournament, with five grandmasters battling against some of the best Estonian masters. Grandmaster Stein, in great form, finished first with 10 points in 13 games. Grandmaster Tal and I tied for second with 9½ points.

Following is one example of the many interesting fighting games played at this tournament.

White: Paul Keres
Black: A. Lutikov

Ruy Lopez

1	e4	e5
2	Nf3	Nc6
3	Bb5	a6
4	Ba4	d6

The Steinitz Defense Deferred has become popular again recently, mainly because of its solid positional foundation. Black gets a slightly cramped position, but he will have good counterchances in the middle-game and no weaknesses.

Curiously, very few players today play 5 Bxc6 + bxc6 6 d4, though theory considers it one of the best lines for White.

5	0-0	Ne7

A rather unusual move but not a bad one. The idea is to bring this knight to g6 to protect the important central square e5.

At one time 5 . . . Bg4 6 h3 h5 was thought to be best for Black, but it is now considered too risky.

6	d4	

I believe this pawn sacrifice is perfectly justified. After 6 . . . b5 7 Bb3 Nxd4 *(7 . . . exd4 8 Ng5!)* 8 Nxd4 exd4 White gets a strong initiative with 9 a4!, and in most cases White regains the pawn with the better game. With his aggressive style, Lutikov does not want to undertake a difficult passive defense.

6 . . .	Ng6
7 c4	

This looks a little more aggressive than the usual 7 c3. By playing his knight to e7 and then to g6, Black showed that he intended to hold the strongpoint e5 at any cost. Since I didn't have to worry about the exchange . . . exd4, I had no need to support d4 with a pawn on c3.

Now, given favorable circumstances, White is prepared to play d5 followed by c5, with an initiative on the queenside.

7 . . .	Bd7
8 Nc3	Be7
9 dxe5	

White had a difficult decision to make. One plan is to proceed 9 d5 Nb8 10 b4, followed by Be3 and c5, starting action on the queenside. In that case the game would have the character of the King's Indian Defense, in which Black would have chances on the other wing with . . . f5.

The text, on the other hand, keeps the position a little more open. White will get use of the open d-file, his knight will occupy the strongpoint d5, and his pieces will have more freedom.

Both plans have their merits; the choice will ultimately be a matter of taste.

9 ...   Ngxe5

I would prefer 9 ... dxe5, since Black's knight stands well on g6 while White's on f3 blocks the queen's path to the kingside.

10 Nxe5   dxe5

White gets the better game also after 10 ... Nxe5 11 Bxd7 + Qxd7 12 b3 followed by Bb2.

In this relatively quiet position, White has only slight positional advantages, and it would seem that Black should have little trouble equalizing completely. Although that may be objectively true, experience has taught me that Black will have to play very carefully and precisely to equalize fully, since the slightest inaccuracy can lead to very unpleasant consequences for him. In practice, positions like this are lost more often than you might think, especially by players who try to avoid a purely defensive game.

11 Be3   0-0
12 Nd5   Rc8

I cannot agree with this move. Black's idea is obvious: He wants to ease his cramped position by playing . . . Bg5, and he needs to have his c-pawn protected in case White exchanges bishops. But Black's idea can be easily thwarted, and the move . . . Rc8 in no way improves his position.

The general rule in cramped positions like this is, of course, to try to ease the pressure by exchanging pieces. But this must be done judiciously. Black chooses the wrong way and soon gets into trouble.

The strange-looking retreat 12 . . . Nb8! looks to me like the right idea, since it improves the positions of Black's pieces. If White wants to avoid exchanges and retreats his bishop by 13 Bc2, Black can choose between 13 . . . b5 and 13 . . . Be6 followed by 14 . . . Nd7, preparing . . . c6. It is only by such careful play that Black can ultimately equalize.

13 Qh5   g6
14 Qf3

This is probably not the most exact retreat, because now Black will get some tactical counterplay. 14 Qe2 seems better, since then 14 . . . Nd4 15 Bxd4 exd4 16 Bxd7 Qxd7 17 Rad1 eventually wins the d-pawn.

14 . . .   b5

Although this leads to a difficult game for Black, it must be considered his best practical chance. At least he will get out of his cramped position, and White will have to play with great determination to exploit his advantages.

Bad, of course, is 14 .. Nd4 15 Bxd4 exd4 16 Bxd7 Qxd7 17 Rfd1, winning the d-pawn.

15 cxb5   axb5

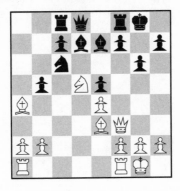

16 Bxb5!

As Spielmann wrote a long time ago, sometimes you *must* sacrifice or your advantage will disappear. That is exactly the situation White is in. The text sacrifices the exchange in return for a promising attack position. The modest retreat 16 Bb3 leads to an acceptable position for Black after 16 . . . Nd4.

16 . . .	Nd4
17 Bxd4	Bxb5
18 Bxe5	Bxf1
19 Rxf1	

The winning variation 19 Nf6 + Bxf6 20 Bxf6 Be2? 21 Qf4! is very nice, but after 20 . . . Qd2! 21 Rxf1 Rfe8 Black's defense would be easier than it is in the game.

Now let's see the result of White's sacrifice. His two good pawns for the exchange are sufficient material compensation, his positional superiority remains intact, and it will not be easy for Black to parry the ominous threats to his king. This is a particularly

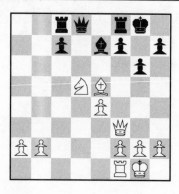

unpleasant situation for an aggressive player like Grandmaster Lutikov, who hates passive defensive positions.

19 . . .   f6

Plausible and probably best, since 19 . . . c6 20 Nf6+ Bxf6 21 Bxf6 and 22 Rd1 leads to an overwhelming position for White. But the text move further weakens Black's king position, and that finally proves to be fatal.

20 Bc3   c6
21 Nf4   Rf7
22 h4!

Black has managed to drive his opponent's well-placed pieces from their dominating positions in the center, but now he will have problems with his king. The h-pawn threatens to tear open the king's protective ring, and if White is also able to play e5 and open the long diagonal for his bishop, Black will be even worse off. So he understandably tries to control e5, but that leads to new trouble around g6.

It's hard to say whether Black has a theoretically

adequate defense, but for practical purposes his position must be considered very difficult and probably lost.

22 ...	Bd6
23 h5	Qc7?

This makes White's task easier, but Black's life is difficult in any case, Lutikov's move prepares a nice tactical defense: 24 hxg6 hxg6 25 Nxg6 Bh2+ 26 Kh1 Rh7, threatening to win with 27 ... Bg1+!. Although even then White has a sufficient defense in 27 Qg4!, he has no need to plunge into such murky complications.

On 23 ... Bxf4 Black gets some counterchances after 24 Qxf4 with 24 ... gxh5 25 e5 Qd5! 26 exf6 Re8, but 24 hxg6! hxg6 25 Qxf4 gives him unsolvable problems. If 25 ... Qe7 26 Qg4 wins a pawn, or if 25 ... Qf8 the answer 26 e5 is very annoying.

Also inadequate is 23 ... g5 because of 24 Ne6 followed by Nd4-f5, but it was probably Black's best practical chance. In fact, Black would have survived longer with any of these defenses than with the one he chose.

	24 Ne6	Qd7

Or 24 . . . Qe7 25 hxg6 hxg6 26 Qg4, and the unprotected rook on c8 could prove fatal.

	25 hxg6	hxg6
	26 Qg4	Kh7

On 26 . . . g5, the answer 27 Qf5 decides.

27 Bxf6!

This ends matters: 27 . . . Rxf6 28 Ng5 + .

	27 . . .	Bf4
	28 Qxf4	Black resigned

A nice little game, quite enjoyable and easy to understand.

(January 1972)

MIDDLEGAME
MASTERPIECES

PART II

BOTVINNIK
BOTCHES A BRILLIANCY
(BUT WINS ANYWAY)

Botvinnik vs. Larsen; Reti Opening
Palma de Mallorca 1967

Judging by achievement in international competition, 1967 was undoubtedly Bent Larsen's year. His results early in the year were not outstanding—a tie for third in Stockholm, fourth place in Beverwijk, a tie for third in Monaco, and a tie for second in Dundee. But those events were just warm-ups for his great achievements in the second half of the year: first prizes in very strong fields in Havana, the Sousse Interzonal, and Palma de Mallorca, and a tie for first in Winnipeg. The Danish grandmaster's splendid results in those events far outshone those of any of his rivals in recent years.

Larsen spent the entire year playing chess, taking part in eight tournaments between January and December. Opinions differ as to the advisability of playing so much. Some think it's too exhausting and can cause a player to lose his taste for chess. Others have just the opposite opinion: that good form can be achieved only by playing often and against a variety of opponents. I'm inclined to agree with the second opinion. A chess master must play as often as his age and health permit.

In Palma de Mallorca, his last tournament of the year, Larsen had a particularly tough struggle. He began extremely well, and with four rounds to go enjoyed a 1½-point lead over two world champions, Botvinnik and Smyslov. But then he had to face Botvinnik—always an unpleasant opponent for him, especially with the white pieces—needing a draw to practically insure a first-place finish.

The importance of this game, particularly at such a late stage of the tournament, placed an enormous nervous strain on both players, who were already exhausted by their strenuous battles in earlier rounds. This helps to explain the errors committed by both sides, errors we are not accustomed to seeing from players of that class.

This hard-fought battle, full of combinational motifs, is just the kind of game chess fans like to see between grandmasters.

White: Mikhail Botvinnik
Black: Bent Larsen

Reti Opening

1	c4	Nf6
2	Nf3	e6

The first indication that Larsen is not aggressively inclined in this game. Normally he prefers the King's Indian with 2 . . . g6.

3	g3	d5
4	Bg2	Be7
5	0-0	0-0
6	b3	

This usually doesn't give Black many problems, but it can still lead to a full game if White avoids simplifications. Transposing to the Catalan Opening with 6 d4 would make things more difficult for Black.

6	. . .	c5
7	Bb2	Nc6
8	e3	

The modern way of playing this opening. White prevents . . . d4 and avoids the early exchange 8 cxd5, which leads to simplifications after 8 . . . Nxd5 9 Nc3 Bf6, etc.

The weakness on d3 that this move creates is of no consequence.

8	. . .	b6
9	Nc3	Bb7
10	d3	Rc8

Black can try 10 . . . dxc4 11 bxc4 Nb4, but it doesn't work because of 12 Qb3!. Since neither 12 . . . Qxd3 13 Ne5 nor 12 . . . Nxd3 13 Rad1 is acceptable for Black, the whole maneuver is a waste of time.

11	Rc1	Rc7

A good plan. Black creates the possibility of bringing the queen to an active position on a8, which also makes room for the rooks to get to the central files. It seems Black will have no problems in this opening.

> 12 Qe2   Rd7
> 13 Rfd1   Re8

But this must be questioned. Black, apparently unaware of any danger, wants to get his pieces to their most active positions before moving his queen to a8. But as Botvinnik's reply shows, Larsen should have played that move immediately, which would have left him with a fully satisfactory game.

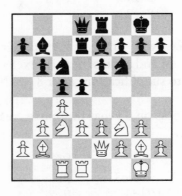

14 cxd5!

Now is the right time to play this move, since Black can't recapture with 14 ... exd5 because of 15 Bh3!; for instance, 15 ... d4 16 Bxd7 dxc3 17 Bxc6 cxb2 18 Bxb7 bxc1Q 19 Rxc1 with a sound extra pawn and the better position for White. The opening of the center gives White some advantage.

14 ...	Nxd5
15 Nxd5	Rxd5

Now 15 ... exd5 16 d4 leads to a clearly inferior position for Black.

16 d4

Black is beginning to have problems in the center. He must reckon with such attacking possibilities as e4, Ne5, and even dxc5, which would bring the white pieces favorably into action. Black would not have these problems if he had already moved his queen to a8.

16 ...	Qa8
17 dxc5	

Black was ready for 17 Ne5, which would have allowed 17 ... Nxe5 18 Bxd5 Bxd5 19 dxe5 Bf3; and 17 e4 leads to nothing after 17 ... Rdd8. But the text move gives White some advantage because of the disruption of Black's queenside pawn formation.

17 ...	Rxd1+
18 Rxd1	Bxc5?

A move like this—removing the last defending piece from the kingside—is suicide, and Larsen must have known it as well as his opponent did. Either he overlooked something or was too optimistic in refusing to allow his queenside pawn structure to be ruined. Optimism is sometimes useful, but it should be taken in reasonable doses.

19 Ng5!

This attacking move is decisive. White's position has all he could wish for: every piece is well posted for attack, he controls the open d-file and the invasion point d7, and the black king is all alone without the support of a single piece. It is not necessary to calculate variations or to analyze deeply to realize that Black's position is very nearly hopeless.

$$19 \ldots \qquad h6$$

Due to the terrible threat of 20 Qh5, this is almost forced. 19 . . . Rd8 20 Bxc6! Bxc6 21 Rxd8+ Qxd8 22 Qh5 loses at once.

$$20 \ Ne4 \qquad Bf8?$$

Larsen is unrecognizable in this game. He is known to be ingenious and stubborn in the defense of difficult positions, but this time his nerves must have gotten the better of him. His move takes care of the threat 21 Qg4, but it completely ignores another, equally devastating threat that makes his position indefensible.

Though Black's position is far from pleasant, he can still offer stubborn resistance with 20 . . . Ne7!. Of course, White would still have much the better of it after 21 Qg4 Ng6 22 Rd7; e.g., 22 . . . Bd5 23 Nxc5 Bxg2 24 Nxe6! Rxe6 (24 . . . Bh1 25 Nf4) 25 Qd4 and wins. But Black can try to improve the defense with 22 . . . Bc6 instead of 22 . . . Bd5, and if 23 Rc7, only then 23 . . . Bd5.

Also better than the text is 20 . . . Be7 21 Qg4 e5, although 22 Nd6 Bxd6 23 Rxd6 leaves White with a clear advantage. In either case, although Black would not be terribly happy, at least he would not yet be staring at mate!

21 Rd7?

So far Botvinnik has conducted the game excellently and achieved a completely won position, and now he could settle matters with the simple combination 21 Nf6 + ! gxf6 22 Qg4 + Kh7 (*22 . . . Bg7 23 Bxf6*) 23 Rd7!, etc. For instance, 23 . . . Re7 24 Be4 + f5 25 Bxf5 + exf5 26 Qxf5 + Kg8 27 Qf6 Kh7 28 Rxe7; or 23 . . . Be7 24 Be4 + Kh8 25 Rxe7.

The two players must have been either extremely tense due to the importance of this game or completely exhausted by the long, tough tournament. In the last three rounds, Botvinnik could achieve only three draws, and Larsen was beaten even by International Master Medina.

21 . . .   f5?

Larsen, perhaps now noticing the above possibility, does not risk provoking it with 21 . . . Re7; for instance, 22 Nf6 + ! Kh8 23 Qc2 gxf6 24 Bxf6 + Kg8 25 Be4 Bg7 26 Bxe7 and wins.

But this move is equally hopeless. The only way to

continue the fight is 21 . . . e5!, having in mind the defense 22 . . . Re7 or 22 . . . Re6.

22 Nd6

White has three winning lines here, one of which begins with the move played. The others, though less forcing; are clear enough:

A) 22 Nf6 + ! gxf6 23 Qh5 Re7 24 Qg6 + and now 24 . . . Bg7 25 Bxc6 Rxd7 26 Bxd7 Bh1 27 Bxe6 + Kh8 28 f3! leads to an easy win for White, as does 24 . . . Rg7 25 Rxg7 + Bxg7 26 Bxc6 Bxc6 27 Bxf6 Qf8 28 Bxg7.

B) 22 Qh5! Re7 23 Rxe7 Nxe7 (better is *23 . . . Bxe7 24 Qg6 Qf8 25 Qxe6 + Qf7* and Black is only a pawn down) 24 Nd6! Bxg2 25 Qf7 + ! Kh7 26 Bxg7! Bxg7 27 Ne8 and wins. Botvinnik said later that he did not see the sacrifice 26 Bxg7! during his calculations.

22 ...	Bxd6
23 Rxd6?	

But this is inexcusable. A simple win is 23 Rxg7 + Kf8 24 Rh7!, and Black is defenseless against the threat 25 Qh5 (*24 . . . Kg8 25 Qh5!*).

23 ...	Nd4!

This is certainly Black's best practical chance. After 23 . . . Re7, the answer 24 Qc4 is decisive (*24 . . . Na5 25 Qd4*), and 23 . . . Nb8 is met by 24 Qh5 Re7 25 Rd8 + Kh7 26 Bh3.

24 Rxd4	Bxg2
25 Rd7	Bh3

Again Larsen finds his best chance. He cannot protect g7, since 25 . . . e5 loses at once to 26 Qc4 + Kh8 27 Qf7. The other possibility, 25 . . . Bh1, also loses quickly after 26 Rxg7 + Kf8 27 f3!; e.g., 27 . . . Qxf3 28 Qd2 Qd5 29 Qb4 + Qc5 30 Qxc5 + bxc5 31 Kxh1; or 27 . . . Bxf3 28 Qb5! Qc6 (or *28 . . . Qd5 29 Rg8 + !*) 29 Qe5 and wins.

26 f3!

A fine move, much better than 26 Rxg7 + Kf8 and only then 27 f3. The difference will be seen on the next move.

26 . . .   Rd8
27 Rxg7 +

Former World Champion Smyslov showed an easy win with 27 Qd1! Rxd7 28 Qxd7 Qf8 29 Qxa7 b5 30 a4 and the a-pawn will decide, since the black queen is helplessly tied to g7 and the bishop is completely useless.

The text move makes matters much more complicated. Both players were already short of time.

27 . . .	Kf8
28 Rh7	

White still has a won game, as his king is much better protected and Black is, in effect, playing without his bishop. The very unpleasant threat now is 29 Rxh6 and the bishop is lost.

28 . . .	Qd5
29 Kf2	Qd1
30 Rh8 +	

Here Smyslov suggested that 30 Bc3! was much stronger because Black can't play 30 . . . Qh1 31 Rh8 + Ke7 32 Bb4 +, etc., and otherwise there is no good defense to the threat of 31 Rxh6. The exchange of rooks makes Black's defense much easier.

30 . . .	Kf7
31 Rxd8	Qxd8
32 Qc2	Qd5

Both players were in serious time trouble. Otherwise, Black probably would have chosen the more prudent 32 . . . Qd6. But the move played is acceptable.

33 Qc7 +	Ke8
34 Qb8 +	

It's difficult for White to create effective threats because his own king's position is too unsafe. For instance, 34 Bd4 is met by 34 . . . Qb5 35 Qb8 + Kd7 36 Qxa7 + Kc6 37 Qa8 + Kc7 with the threat of mate on f1. But maybe that line, continuing 38 Ke1, is still White's best chance to win. After the move in the game, Black can force the exchange of queens.

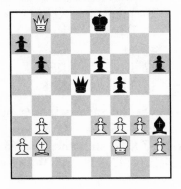

34 ...   Kd7??

In time trouble, Larsen gives up another pawn, and that means a hopeless ending. Correct, of course, is 34 ... Qd8, forcing the exchange of queens, after which it is very doubtful whether White has any real winning chances. Now the game is virtually over.

35 Qxa7+   Kc8

Slightly better is 35 ... Ke8 to avoid trading queens now that he is two pawns down.

36 Qa6+   Kc7
37 Qc4+

The simplest way, although 37 Bd4 is also very strong.

37 ...   Qxc4
38 bxc4   Kc6

The ending is hopeless for Black. White easily creates a passed pawn on the queenside, after which his only problem will be getting one on the other side.

39	Bd4	h5
40	a4	Kc7
41	c5	bxc5
42	Bxc5	Kc6
43	Bb4	Kb6

After 43 . . . e5, the same winning line as in the game is possible: 44 g4 hxg4 45 Kg3 e4 (*45 . . . f4 + 46 exf4 exf4 + 47 Kh4, and otherwise 46 e4 is threatened*) 46 fxe4 fxe4 47 Kf4 and White gets another passed pawn.

44	g4!	hxg4
45	Kg3	e5
46	e4!	

After the adjournment Botvinnik plays the endgame very precisely. This move wins immediately, since 46 . . . f4 + is met by 47 Kh4.

46	. . .	fxe4
47	fxg4	Black resigned

(*May 1968*)

"CRAZY" BRONSTEIN

Bronstein vs. Tal; King's Gambit
U.S.S.R. Team Championship, 1968

The team championship of the U.S.S.R. consists of two divisions, one for teams representing the several Soviet republics, the other for teams representing various sports clubs. The two divisions play their matches in alternate years.

In 1968, the twelve best sports clubs sent their players to Riga, the capital of Latvia, to fight for the championship. Each team consisted of ten players: five men, two women, two boys, and one girl. With the exception of ex-World Champion Botvinnik and a few players who were competing in a tournament in Palma de Mallorca, all the leading grandmasters of the Soviet Union took part.

The main interest, of course, was focused on the top boards. Although most of the games on those boards were not real fights, some were quite interesting and full of competitive spirit. One of the most sensational games was the encounter between David Bronstein and Mikhail Tal, a complicated battle with many surprises.

White: David Bronstein
Black: Mikhail Tal

King's Gambit

1	e4	e5
2	f4!	

The spectators buzz with excitement: Bronstein is playing the King's Gambit!

Well, that is not so extraordinary—Bronstein has played this opening often of late, as has Bobby Fischer in both American and international tournaments. Objectively, it is neither better nor worse than many other openings commonly played in modern tournaments. It is, however, out of fashion.

The reason for the audience's excitement was not that Bronstein was playing this opening but that he was playing it against Tal. I heard somebody say that he must be crazy to use this opening against the world's greatest living combinative player.

Crazy or not, Bronstein has chosen it, and the result is one of the most beautiful and exciting games played between leading grandmasters in recent years.

2 . . .   d5

Tal refuses the pawn offer by offering one himself with the Falkbeer Countergambit. The King's Gambit seems to cast a spell on those who have to face it: Almost everyone feels that accepting the gambit with 2 . . . exf4 is too risky, and sometimes they decline it in obviously inferior ways.

3 exd5	e4
4 d3	Nf6
5 dxe4	

White has many ways to continue. This is one of the oldest and perhaps one of the best.

5 ...	Nxe4
6 Nf3	Bc5
7 Qe2	Bf5!

All according to well-known theory, which tells us that the alternatives—7 . . . f5 8 Be3, 7 . . . Qxd5 8 Nfd2!, and 7 . . . Bf2+ 8 Kd1 Qxd5+ 9 Nfd2—lead to advantage for White. The move played was introduced by Dr. Tarrasch in Mährisch-Ostrow 1923 against Spielmann. The idea is that after 8 g4? 0-0! 9 gxf5 Re8, Black gets a very strong attack for the sacrificed piece.

8 Nc3	Qe7
9 Be3	

This position, too, is well-known to theory. Black's best line here is thought to be 9 . . . Bxe3 10 Qxe3 Nxc3 11 Qxe7+ Kxe7 12 bxc3 and now 12 . . . Bxc2 or 12 . . . Be4 with an acceptable game.

9 . . .   Nxc3?

The books do not sanction this move, and since Tal has no improvement in mind (as we will see), there is no reason to remove the customary question mark.

This is a good example of the advantage that can be obtained by choosing an unfashionable opening. Most modern masters study all the popular opening systems thoroughly and analyze almost every possibility in every variation, many of which extend deep into the middlegame. Thus they avoid having to create anything over the board but can simply repeat their home analysis. When such a theory-oriented player encounters a new situation in an actual game, however, he often fails to find the right continuation because he is not used to making decisions in unfamiliar positions. Often he will prefer a safe, not-to-lose move, and then, after the game, will study the situation at home and prepare for the next time.

As we can see, the importance of opening preparation at home is often overestimated, while the ability to solve new problems satisfactorily over the board is not sufficiently cultivated.

I certainly do not include Tal among players who cannot find their way in relatively unknown positions. But the fact that even Tal can be led astray speaks in favor of the policy of choosing lesser-known opening variations.

What a pity it would be if a game of chess actually began with the middlegame!

10 Bxc5	Nxe2
11 Bxe7	Nxf4
12 Ba3!	

Also good is 12 Bg5 Nxd5 13 0-0-0, with a fine

position for the pawn, but Bronstein's move looks even stronger. Black can win a pawn now with 12 . . . Nxd5, but that would leave White with a great advantage in development and Black would have trouble castling on either side.

Of course, 12 . . . Bxc2 is out of the question because of 13 Rc1 followed by Rxc7.

12 . . .   Nd7?

As long ago as 1924, Tartakower's massive work on the openings, *Die Hypermoderne Schachpartie*, pointed out the variation 12 . . . Nxd5 13 0-0-0, with the better game for White. Tal is understandably eager to bring his king to safety, and so he prepares . . . 0-0-0, but his idea is flawed by a miscalculation and cannot be carried out.

He should choose Tartakower's recommendation followed by 13 . . . Be6, intending to return the extra pawn to complete his development.

Now his position becomes very difficult.

13   0-0-0

Suddenly Tal became very agitated and spent almost an hour thinking about his reply. Only now did he notice that his intended 13 . . . 0-0-0 would be a grave mistake that would lose a piece after 14 Rd5! followed by the surprising point 15 g4!. But if Black can't castle, his previous move made no sense, and now he is in real trouble.

13 . . .   Be4

There is no adequate defense against the many threats—14 Rd4, 14 Re1 +, 14 Nd4, etc. This move is an attempt to salvage a somewhat acceptable game.

14 Ng5

White had many strong continuations, such as 14
Rd4 f5 15 Ng5, or if 14 . . . Bxf3 15 gxf3; or 14 Re1
f5 15 Ng5, etc. The text move isn't bad either, but it
somehow complicates matters.

14 . . .   Bxd5

15 g3!!

The most unexpected move, and typically Bronstein! Few players would even consider a move like 15
g3 here, especially since White has plenty of other
promising continuations. Simply 15 Re1+ is very
strong, and after 15 . . . Kd8 or 15 . . . Be6, only then
16 g3!, etc. The move 15 g3 deserves two exclamation points not only because it is so strong but also
because it is so original and so extraordinarily surprising.

When I asked Bronstein after the game why he did
not play 15 Re1+ first, he looked at me as if I could
not understand anything about the position, and said,
"I could not miss the opportunity to play a move like
15 g3 against Tal, which I may not have again in my
whole life."

That's Bronstein. I'm glad he played 15 g3, for it leads to very interesting complications.

15 ...   Bxh1
16 gxf4   c5!

Black has little choice. White was threatening to win at once with 17 Re1 +, and 17 Bc4 and Bh3 were strong threats, too. He could have tried 16 ... 0-0-0, but after 17 Bh3 Bc6 18 Nxf7 he would have a very cramped position with no counterplay.

The text move closes the terrible diagonal a3-f8 and gives Black chances for a successful defense, but his position is still difficult.

17 Bc4

The continuation 17 Bh3 Bc6 18 Re1 + Kf8 is not decisive, nor is 17 Re1 + Kf8 18 Bc4 Bc6 19 Nxf7 b5!, with counterplay for Black.

17 ...   Bc6
18 Nxf7

It would have been pleasant to give mate by 18 Bxf7 + Kf8? 19 Rxd7! Bxd7 20 Bxc5, but Black would play 18 ... Ke7 and if 19 Re1 + Kd6, etc.

Black cannot play 18 ... Rf8 here because of 19 Re1 +, but he has other ways of making his opponent's task difficult.

18 ...   b5!

This saves the exchange, since 19 Nxh8 bxc4 leaves White's knight trapped on h8. As is now apparent, 15 g3, though beautiful, did not make White's task any easier.

19 Nd6+   Ke7
20 Nxb5

White still has a nice game. His two bishops, a
solid pawn for the exchange, and Black's exposed
king give him a slight superiority, but by no means
should his chances be overestimated.

We all know how hard it is to adapt to a sudden
change in circumstances. Having obtained some
chances to save his lost game, Tal misses the right
defense and gets a lost position again.

20 . . .   Rhf8?

He should simplify the situation with 20 . . . Bxb5!
21 Bxb5 Rhd8. Although White would still have two
bishops and a pawn for a rook and a knight, Black's
position would be not at all hopeless. With careful
defense he would have good chances to save the game.

21 Nd4!

Tal must have overlooked this strong reply. He
can't protect the bishop, since 21 . . . Rf6 is met by 22

Nxc6+ Rxc6 23 Bd5, and 21 ... Rac8 is met by 22
Nxc6+ Rxc6 23 Bb5 or simply 23 Re1+. There's a
nice mate after 21 ... Bb7 22 Re1+ Kd6 23 Nb5+
and 24 Re6 mate.

21 ...	Bg2
22 Ne6	Rf5

On 22 ... Rf6, the capture 23 Nxc5 is enough to
win.

23 Rg1

Having already spent a great deal of time on the
first part of the game, both opponents are now forced
to play virtually move-on-move. This explains the inaccuracies in the second part. Very strong here is 23
b4!; since Black can't take the pawn, White wins the
c-pawn with continuing pressure.

23 ...	Be4
24 Nc7	

It's good tactics in time pressure to make moves the
opponent doesn't expect. Though the text move isn't
bad, 24 Rxg7+ Kd6 25 Rxd7+ Kxd7 26 Nxc5+
Rxc5 27 Bxc5 wins fairly easily.

24 ...	Rd8
25 Rxg7+	Kf6

Better is 25 ... Kd6 26 Nb5+ Kc6 27 Nxa7+
Kb6 28 Be6 Rxf4! with complications. But instead of
26 Nb5+ White can play, of course, 26 Ne6 Re8 27
Nd4 Rxf4 28 Nb5+, etc., winning the a-pawn under
more advantageous circumstances. Even after the text
move, White can take a pawn with impunity by 26
Rxh7.

26 Rf7+	Kg6
27 Re7	Nf6
28 Ne6	Rc8

On 28 ... Re8, the maneuver 29 Rg7+ Kh6 30 Rg1, threatening 31 Ng7 or 31 Bxc5 or 31 Nxc5, is very annoying. Now White takes a moment to activate his queen bishop.

| 29 b3 | Rh5 |
| 30 Ng5 | Bd5 |

Black is obviously lost. There's no point in criticizing the players' moves in time pressure, where anything can happen.

31 Bd3+	Kh6
32 Bb2	c4
33 Bf5	

There's nothing wrong with the simple 33 bxc5, of course, but the text is simple, too.

33 ...	c3
34 Bxc8	cxb2+
35 Kxb2	Rxh2
36 Rxa7	Rf2

This must have been something for the spectators! Black simply doesn't have time to resign!

37 Ra4	Kg6
38 Rd4	h5
39 a4	h4
40 a5	

It almost looks like a real race to see whose pawn will queen first!

It seems to me that today's masters and grandmasters do not use their time in the best way. What good is it to play the first part of a game well and then spoil it by playing lightning chess in the second part? I think it would be better if the first part were played somewhat less deeply so that the opponents would have time to conduct the second part in an acceptable manner.

40 . . .	Bg2
41 a6	Nh5
42 Bb7	Nxf4

They don't even notice that it's the forty-second move and that the time control has been passed!

| 43 Rxf4 | Black resigned |

(March 1969)

GAME 5

OLD FRIENDS IN A "FRIENDLY" GAME

**Keres vs. Mikenas; Alekhine's Defense
U.S.S.R. Team Championship, Riga 1968**

Vladas Mikenas and I have known each other for about forty years. He has been my second in a number of difficult tournament battles, and apart from chess we have been friends for many years.

We first had the pleasure of fighting against each other at the Warsaw Olympiad in 1935, and since then we have had many interesting battles. Our most recent game was at the U.S.S.R. Team Championship in Riga. Since we are both in our "comfortable" years now, we generally prefer to avoid fierce fighting games in favor of quieter, solid play, where experience counts more than calculation. But in this game complications unexpectedly arose, resulting in the kind of combinative game we might have played thirty years ago. Look what can happen when two old lions get mad at each other!

White: Paul Keres
Black: Vladas Mikenas

Alekhine's Defense

1 e4	Nf6
2 Nc3	

Mikenas is one of the best experts on Alekhine's Defense and has achieved excellent results with this rare opening. At the start of this game I was rather peaceably inclined and had no great ambition in the opening.

2 ...	d5
3 exd5	Nxd5
4 Nge2	

This may be a new move, but it is certainly no "refutation" of Black's opening system. It is neither better nor worse than any other developing move, and leaves Black a wide choice of good plans.

4 ...	Bg4

I cannot endorse this move. The bishop will be badly placed on g4, allowing White to gain extra developing tempi. Black had several good choices, among them 4 ... g6 and even 4 ... e5.

5 h3	Nxc3
6 bxc3	

If the purpose of Black's fourth move was to prevent 6 Nxc3 and the normal development of White's pieces, it must be considered a failure. The weakening of White's pawn structure is not significant, and in fact Black will have a more serious problem trying to

neutralize his opponent's pressure along the open
b-file.

6 . . .   Bf5

Nor is this move the best. The retreat 6 . . . Bh5 is
dubious because of 7 c4 followed by 8 g4 and 9 Bg2,
or even 7 g4 Qd5 8 Rg1 Bg6 9 Bg2.

If Black, having played the unfortunate 4 . . . Bg4,
wants to keep his bishop, 6 . . . Bc8 is relatively best.
But the most normal move is 6 . . . Bxe2 7 Bxe2 c6,
with only a slightly better game for White.

7 Rb1   Qd5

Active defense does not lead to a satisfactory result
here, so 7 . . . Qc8 should have been preferred.

8 Ng3

Simple and good, but for a long time I considered
the interesting pawn sacrifice 8 c4!? Qxc4 9 Nc3
Qe6+ 10 Be2 followed by 11 0-0 with a very fine
game. It was hard to decide whether that move or the
one I chose would be more effective.

8 . . .   Bc8

Thus Black admits that his opening strategy was
faulty. Too risky, of course, is 8 . . . Qxa2 9 Rxb7
Qxc2 10 Bb5 +.

9 c4   Qa5
10 Bb2!   c6

Black is badly behind in development, and the capture 10 . . . Qxa2 11 Bd3 followed by 12 0-0 would
only have made it worse.

| 11 | Bc3 | Qc7 |
| 12 | Bd3 | |

White wants to exploit the strength of his well-developed pieces without the pawns getting in their way. But 12 d4 followed by 13 Bd3 and 14 0-0 is also good.

| 12 | ... | e5 |

This gives White a good target to attack, but otherwise Black can't develop his pieces. Now the game enters a very interesting phase.

| 13 | 0-0 | f6 |

This kind of position, rarely seen today, recalls the games of the last century. White has developed all his pieces while Black has made only pawn moves and brought out his queen. Such a big advantage in time usually offers opportunities for various combinations and sacrifices.

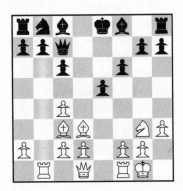

14 f4!

A simple rule advises that if you have an advantage in development you should open the position. Black can't play 14 . . . exf4, of course, because of 15 Qh5 + or 15 Nh5 with decisive threats. So he intends to base his defense on maintaining the stronghold on e5, making use of the fact that when the white pawn gets to e5 it will be pinned against the undefended knight on g3. But, as I said before, positions like this always offer possibilities for combinative solutions.

| 14 . . . | Be6 |
| 15 fxe5 | Nd7 |

If it were Black's move here, he would get a reasonable game by capturing . . . Nxe5 or bringing his king to safety with . . . 0-0-0. Unfortunately for Black, it is White's move.

I spent a lot of time trying to decide on the simplest way of realizing my advantage. The most obvious idea is the sacrifice 16 exf6, but I had to calculate other attractive possibilities, too.

First, 16 Ne4, to answer 16 . . . Nxe5 with 17 Nxf6 + gxf6 18 Rxf6 with a winning position, or 16 . . . fxe5 17 Ng5. Second, 16 Nh5, which after 16 . . . Nxe5 17 Nxf6 + leads to the above variation, and in case of 16 . . . fxe5 allows the sacrifice 17 Nxg7 + ! Bxg7 18 Qh5 + and 19 Qg5 +, etc.

Although I realized that both of those continuations were very strong and good enough to win eventually, I decided not to allow Black the opportunity for the pawn sacrifice 16 . . . 0-0-0, which would give him some counterplay after either 16 Ne4 or 16 Nh5. So finally the decision was in favor of the piece sacrifice, perhaps the most convincing line.

16 exf6!   Qxg3
17 fxg7

After 17 Rf3 Black has the defense 17 ... Qg5.
After the text move things look desperate for Black,
since 17 ... Bxg7 18 Qh5+ followed by 19 Rf3
would be hopeless.

Despite his difficult position, Mikenas, ever the excellent tactician, finds a surprising resource that almost gets him out of trouble.

17 ...   Bc5+!
18 Kh1   Rg8

On 18 ... 0-0-0 (with the idea *19 gxh8Q Bd6!*),
White wins easily with 19 Rf3.

19 Qe1

Also good for a win is 19 Qh5+ Kd8 20 Rf3 Qc7
21 Bf5!, but the text looks even more forceful. After
19 ... Qxe1 20 Rbxe1 Ke7 21 Bf5, or 19 ... Qd6 20
Bf5 Ke7 21 Qh4+, White regains his piece with a
couple of extra pawns.

What can Black do now except turn over his king?

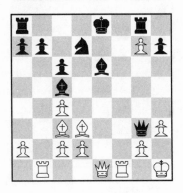

19 . . .   Bd6!

This clever tactical finesse once again demonstrates that there is no limit to the ingenuity of the human mind. Moves like this are the magnets that attract us to the game of chess and win new friends for it.

It's a pity for Mikenas that this move is ultimately not quite sufficient to save the game—he would have deserved it!

20 Qxe6 +

The prosaic winning line is 20 Qxg3 Bxg3 21 Rf3 Be5 22 Re1 Bxc3 23 Rxe6 + Kd8 24 dxc3 Rxg7 25 Rh6, with three extra pawns for the endgame. But I was so fond of the following combination that I decided to find out whether I could still make an accurate calculation after four hours of play.

20 . . .   Kd8
21 Qxg8 +   Kc7

What now?, you may ask. Black threatens mate on h2, the white queen is attacked, and White has no useful check. Is White lost?

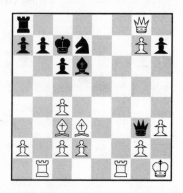

22 Rxb7 + !

No! This is the combination I wanted to try. The next moves are forced.

| 22 ... | Kxb7 |
| 23 Rb1+ | Nb6 |

Black has nothing else. On 23 ... Kc7, the answer 24 Ba5+ Nb6 25 Qf7+ is decisive, and after 23 ... Ka6 24 c5+ Qxd3 25 Qxa8 is good enough.

| 24 Qf7+ | Bc7 |
| 25 Kg1! | |

This is the final point of White's combination. He has a couple of extra pawns, most of Black's pieces are pinned, and Black's queen can't conduct an attack all alone.

Black could have resigned here, but we continued playing because of mutual time trouble.

25 ...	Rd8
26 c5	Rxd3
27 cxd3	Qh2+
28 Kf2	Qg3+
29 Ke2	Black resigned

Here Mikenas smilingly offered his hand. All defending resources are exhausted.

I fully realize that this is no model game, especially in the opening, but it is an entertaining fight of which neither player should feel ashamed. I think games like this are more warmly accepted than typical grandmaster games that are absolutely correct from first move to last.

Thank you, Miki, for this excellent fight!

(August 1969)

GAME 6

NO WAY TO TREAT A GRANDMASTER

Kupreichik vs. Tal, Sicilian Defense
Sochi 1970

Top-ranked grandmasters cannot stay in top form forever. As they grow older and meet younger rivals, their results inevitably suffer. This creates a crucial problem for chess organizations in countries with leading grandmasters: The new generation of younger stars must be encouraged, but how can they be assured of getting the needed experience in strong tournaments and enough opportunities to improve so that, when the time comes, they will be ready to take the places of their older colleagues?

I believe the best way is regular consultation with experienced grandmasters combined with practical play in serious tournaments against opponents of different classes. The young player thus gains valuable insights into the strenuous atmosphere of international tournaments, and familiarity with players of various strengths and styles.

The U.S.S.R. Chess Federation tried a different method: a mixed tournament of masters and grandmasters, which was played in Sochi last October. Seven grandmasters had to play two games each against seven young masters. The grandmasters were Liberzon, Lutikov, Korchnoi, Shamkovich, Stein, Suetin, and Tal; the masters were Gulko, Kupreichik, Kuzmin, Podgaets, Tseshkovsky, Tukmakov, Vaganian, and Belyavsky (the latter two played only seven games apiece). The final score was 51½–46½ in the grandmasters' favor. Tal had the best score among the grandmasters, with 10½ points, and Kuzmin the best among the masters, with 9½.

It was an interesting event, to be sure, but I don't think this sort of contest is really the right way to develop a young player's chess. In a tournament like this, the masters have everything at stake and play with full energy and ambition, while the grandmasters, understandably, have no real interest in the competition. That does not mean that the fine successes achieved by the young players at Sochi were not fully deserved. But how is one to explain that Korchnoi lost half his games—seven in all?

A normal tournament would have been better—and an international tournament better still. An experiment like the one in Sochi could easily lead the young masters to overestimate their abilities, and that, as a practical matter, would mean the end of their development into real grandmasters.

Nevertheless, there were a number of interesting fights at the Sochi tournament, which not only showed the young players' tactical and aggressive qualities but also pointed up the many deficiencies in their play. The following encounter earned a special award as the best attacking game of the tournament.

adimir Kupreichik
khail Tal

Sicilian Defense

1 e4	c5
2 Nf3	d6
3 d4	cxd4
4 Nxd4	Nc6

This rather unusual order of moves permits White
to play 5 c4, but apparently neither Tal nor his opponent thinks very highly of that Maroczy move.

5 Nc3	Nf6
6 Bc4	

This move has become very popular again in recent
years, thanks mainly to the excellent results achieved
with it by Bobby Fischer.

6 . . .	Qb6

In the main line, 6 . . . e6, White usually builds up
a strong attacking position in which the outcome of
the give-and-take battle often depends on a single
tempo. Young masters, as a rule, are very well prepared in theoretical variations—better informed, in
fact, than their older colleagues. It is therefore clear
why Tal chooses a rare continuation here rather than
enter a lengthy theoretical discussion.

7 Nb3

This square is needed for the bishop. 7 Nde2, as
Fischer played against Benko in Bled 1959, looks
more logical.

7 . . .	e6
8 Be3	

Since Black's queen is not well placed where it is, it makes no sense to force it to a better square. Worth considering is 8 0-0 followed by Kh1 and f4, meanwhile keeping the option of Bg5.

8	. . .	Qc7
9	f4	a6
10	Bd3	

It's now clear that the knight on b3 is occupying the bishop's best retreat. A logical move is 10 a4, but then Black gets a good game with 10 . . . Nb4 11 Bd3 e5, or 11 Be2 d5, etc.

10	. . .	b5
11	a3	

This move is often played in such situations, but I don't like it because it weakens the queenside somewhat. It would be a good move if it actually prevented Black from playing both . . . b4 and . . . Nb4, but in this game he is able to play . . . b4 with great effect. The immediate 11 Qf3 seems better.

11	. . .	Be7
12	Qf3	Bb7
13	0-0	Rc8
14	Rae1	0-0
15	Qh3	

Black has achieved a fine game and it's hard for White to find a promising way to begin an attack. The typical 15 g4 is met by 15 . . . b4 16 axb4 Nxb4 17 g5 Nd7, and it is only White who will have trouble with his weakened king position. Nor is 15 Qg3 b4 16 axb4 Nxb4 17 e5 dangerous because of 17 . . . Nh5 18 Qh3 Nxd3 19 cxd3 g6, etc.

15	. . .	b4!

With this strong move Black completes his opening plan and launches a dangerous initiative on the queen-side. Black seems to have emerged from the opening with a very satisfactory position.

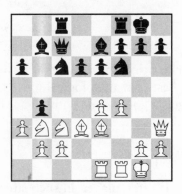

16 Nd5?

Kupreichik himself seems to think the game is running in Black's favor, so he takes the desperate gamble of sacrificing a piece to get an attack going. To make such a sacrifice against a combinative player like Tal shows a lot of youthful enthusiasm! Objectively, however, the sacrifice is quite unsound and offers White nothing more than a few tactical chances of no real value.

Actually, White does not have very pleasant alternatives. The attack 16 axb4 Nxb4 17 e5 dxe5 18 fxe5 leads nowhere after the simple 18 . . . Qxe5!; for instance, 19 Rxf6 Nxd3, or 19 Bd4 Qh5. Also 16 Ne2 bxa3 17 bxa3 g6 looks perfectly satisfactory for Black.

Relatively best is either 16 Na4 or 16 axb4 Nxb4 17 Nd4 with an acceptable game.

16 . . .   exd5

      17 exd5   Nb8
      18 Bd4

White doesn't have time to bring his knight into action, since on 18 Nd4 Black has the simple defense 18 . . . Rcd8!, and if 19 Nf5 Bc8. White must proceed with direct threats.

      18 . . .   g6

Of course not 18 . . . h6? 19 Bxf6 Bxf6 20 Qf5, regaining the piece.

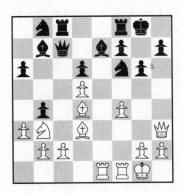

      19 Rf3

White has many ways to continue the attack, though none of them guarantees success. The most plausible attempt is 19 f5, but then 19 . . . Bxd5 20 fxg6 fxg6 is good enough to repulse the attack; e.g., 21 Rxe7 Qxe7 22 Bxf6 Qe6!, and White is left in a hopeless position, as Tal correctly pointed out.

After the game, Kupreichik thought 19 Re3 would have effectively strengthened the attack, since if 19 . . . Bxd5 20 Qh4, and the double threat of 21 Bxf6 and 21 Rxe7 should give White sufficient attacking chances.

Leaving aside the question of whether 19 . . . Bxd5 is Black's best reply, let us consider the position after 20 Qh4. We will soon see that White's threats are not really effective and that Black gets a decisive advantage with the simple 20 . . . Bxb3!.

Now 21 Bxf6 Bxf6 22 Qxf6 Qb6 23 Re1 Rfe8 is definitely bad for White, and after 21 Rxe7 Qxe7 22 Bxf6 Qe3+ 23 Kh1 Nd7, there is no doubt about who has the upper hand. So White is compelled to answer 20 . . . Bxb3 with 21 cxb3.

Now Black can play 21 . . . Bd8, since again 22 Bxf6 Bxf6 23 Qxf6 is bad because of 23 . . . Qb6!, and otherwise Black will consolidate his position with 22 . . . Nbd7 or 22 . . . Nc6. Another possibility is 21 . . . Rce8. But even simpler and more forcing is 21 . . . Nc6! at once.

Here again, 22 Bxf6 Bxf6 23 Qxf6 Qb6 is unacceptable for White, and after 22 Rxe7 Qxe7 23 Bxf6 (23 *Qxf6 Qxf6 24 Bxf6* offers only slight practical chances to save the game) 23 . . . Qe3+ 24 Rf2 (24 *Kh1 Qxd3*) Nd4!, Black wins easily.

So it makes no real difference which rook White plays to the third rank.

19	. . .	Bxd5
20	Rfe3	Bd8
21	Qh4	

Having eliminated the strong pawn on d5, Black was threatening to refute his opponent's attack completely with 21 . . . Nc6. For instance, if 21 Qh6 Nc6 22 Bxf6 Bxf6 23 Rh3 Rfe8 24 Qxh7+ Kf8 with an easy win. To avoid that, White plays a move that forces Black's knight to d7 instead of c6. But this costs White a valuable tempo, and besides, the knight stands quite well on d7.

There is no doubt that Black has refuted his opponent's piece sacrifice and should now have an easy win.

21 . . .   Nbd7

It is also possible to exchange first with 21 . . . Bxb3 22 cxb3 and only now 22 . . . Nbd7.

White's only chance lies in concentrating his forces against the g6 square, though that will take time. Meanwhile, Black must beware also of tactical shots; for instance, 21 . . . Nh5? 22 Qxh5!, or 21 . . . Ne8? 22 Qxh7 + !.

22 Qh6   Qb7

One gets the impression here that Tal was too sure of his victory and did not pay sufficient attention to his opponent's few remaining attacking possibilities. Tal's move is certainly good enough to win, but there are much clearer ways of ending White's dreams of attack.

During the game, Tal considered the surprise move 22 . . . Qb6!?, which, though playable, is by no means necessary and is certainly not the simplest. It seems to me that the clearest continuation for Black is further simplification with 22 . . . Bxb3. After 23 cxb3 (insufficient is *23 Rg3 Bxc2*, adding protection to g6), Black plays 23 . . . Qa5! with the deadly double threat of 24 . . . Qh4 and 24 . . . Bb6. White would have nothing left but to resign.

Now, however, things get a little more complicated.

23 Rg3!

Black must now consider the possibility of a sacrifice on g6, which would lead at least to perpetual check; e.g., 23 . . . Bxb3 24 Bxg6!, etc. He must also pay attention to the possible 24 f5, increasing the pressure on g6.

White has some real threats, and they require exact defense on Black's part.

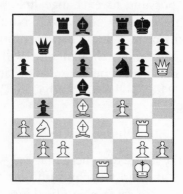

23 . . .   Nc5?

A grave mistake that ignores White's principal threat, the attack against g6.

From the very beginning of the attack, Black's main enemy has been the strong bishop on d4, and he should take the opportunity to eliminate it with 23 . . . Bb6!. White would still have some threats, but with correct defense Black should be able to exploit his material advantage. Let's look at some of the possibilities:

A) 24 Bxg6 Bxd4+ (after *24 . . . fxg6 25 Rxg6+*, White has perpetual check) 25 Nxd4 fxg6 26 Nf5 (hopeless is *26 Re7 Rf7*, or *26 Rxg6+ hxg6 27 Qxg6+ Kh8 28 Qh6+ Nh7*) 26 . . . Ne5! (*26 . . . Rf7 27 Ne7+ Rxe7 28 Rxe7 Bf7* is also good) 27 fxe5 Qa7+ and wins.

B) 24 Re7 (*24 f5* is well answered by *24 . . . Ne5!*)

24 ... Bxd4+ 25 Nxd4 Qb6 26 Bxg6 Qxd4+ 27 Kf1 Kh8! and it's all over.

Very convincing. But now let's look at some of the other variations possible after 24 Re7. Instead of 24 ... Bxd4+, Black can play 24 ... Bxb3 first. Both players thought this would enable White to save the game by means of the following interesting combination: 25 Bxg6! Bxd4+ 26 Kh1 Kh8! 27 Bxf7!.

Position after 27 Bxf7 (analysis)

This looks really strong, threatening mate on g7. The defense 27 ... Rg8 doesn't help because of 28 Bxg8, and 27 ... Ne4? allows the surprising 28 Qxh7+! Kxh7 29 Bg8+ and 30 Rh7 mate! If 27 ... Rxf7 28 Rxf7 wins. Black's only defense, therefore, is 27 ... Ng4!.

Now things look bad for White, since 28 Rxg4 is met simply by 28 ... Rxf7, and after the sacrifice 28 Qxh7+ Kxh7 29 Bd5+ (or *29 Bxb3+*) Kh6! White has nothing. But White has the surprising answer 28 Bg6!, again threatening mate, this time on h7. Since 28 ... Nxh6 29 Rxh7+ Kg8 30 Bd3+ leads to mate, both players thought Black would be forced to take the perpetual check 28 ... Nf2+ 29 Kg1 Ng4+, etc.

But it seems to me that even in this incredibly complicated position (after *28 Bg6*), Black can still win by playing 28 ... Rf7!. Now 29 Rxg4 will be met by 29 ... Rxe7, so White has only 29 Rxf7 Nxh6 30 Rxh7+ Kg8 31 Be4+ Kf8 32 Bxb7, but after 32 ... Rxc2 White would hardly be able to save the game.

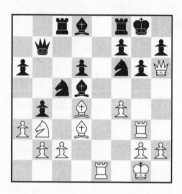

24 Nxc5	dxc5
25 f5!	

Wonderfully played. It won't be easy for Black to avoid a catastrophe on g6.

25 ...	cxd4?

The decisive mistake, after which the game cannot be saved.

Black's only defense is 25 ... Rc7!, so that after 26 fxg6 fxg6 27 Bxg6 hxg6 28 Rxg6+ he has the move 28 ... Rg7!. After 25 ... Rc7!, White must continue 26 Bxc5!, threatening mate on f8.

If now 26 ... Rxc5, then 27 fxg6 decides, as in the game. It's also hard to find an adequate defense for Black after 26 ... Be7 27 Bd4! Bd8 28 Rh3, etc. But with 26 ... Re7! 27 fxg6 fxg6! (*27 ... Rxe1+ 28*

Kf2 leaves Black in trouble), or 27 Bxe7 Bxe7 28 fxg6 fxg6 (*29 Bxg6 Kh8!*), Black can put up a stubborn defense and the outcome of the game would not be at all certain.

We know Tal to be a brilliant attacking player who is virtually unequaled in complicated combinative positions. Here he has a position he should like, but he's on the wrong side! He hates defending so much that even in the kind of position in which he should feel most at home, if he's on the defending side he is surprisingly unsure of himself.

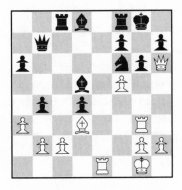

26	fxg6	fxg6
27	Bxg6!	

This is decisive. The bishop can't be taken because of mate in two, and the only defense against the threats of 28 Bxh7+ and 28 Bf7+ is to give up the rook. But this restores material equality while leaving White with his strong attacking position.

27	...	Kh8
28	Qxf8+	Ng8

No great difference is made by 28 ... Bg8 29 Bf5,

threatening 30 Bxc8 and 30 Re8. Black's move is a last attempt at a swindle—for instance, 29 Be4 d3!, threatening 30 . . . Bb6 +—but White keeps it simple.

29 Bf5!

Now the rook can't leave the eighth rank because the bishop on d8 needs protection, so White wins the decisive tempo to renew his threats.

29 . . .	Rb8
30 Re8	Qf7
31 Rh3!	Black resigned

The simplest and prettiest way to end the game. Since mate can be avoided only at great material cost, Black gave up.

The conclusion was very nice indeed, with an excellently conducted attack by Kupreichik. Although there may be some question about whether the game as a whole deserved the honor of a special prize as best attacking game, I hope readers enjoyed it as much as I enjoyed analyzing it.

(May 1971)

BETWEEN CALCULATION AND INTUITION

Keres vs. Westerinen; Alekhine's Defense
Tallinn 1971

The Tallinn International Tournament, held in February and March 1971, was quite a strong and interesting event. The field included eight international grandmasters and representatives from eight countries.

It was a pleasure to meet two players from the United States, Grandmaster Arthur Bisguier and International Master Anthony Saidy, the first American players to visit the Soviet Union in a long time. I understand that their participation would have been quite difficult without the most kind cooperation of the U.S. Chess Federation and of Mr. Edmondson[1]

---

[1]Ed Edmondson was then the Executive Director of the U.S. Chess Federation.

personally. I hope this visit will pave the way for further exchanges of players between our two countries.

All the players seemed more interested in having a good time than in struggling for points. The result was a tournament full of lively fighting games with many fine points (as well as flaws)—so many interesting games, in fact, that it was very hard to choose only one for *Chess Life & Review* readers. I finally chose a game of my own, not because I considered it better than the others but because I was so familiar with everything that happened in it and because I enjoyed it very much. I hope you will like it too.

White: Paul Keres
Black: Heikki Westerinen

Alekhine's Defense

1	e4	Nf6
2	e5	Nd5
3	Nc3	

The study of chess openings nowadays stretches deep into the middlegame, and some of the newer variations are analyzed as far as the twentieth move. From the standpoint of exploring the openings and enriching theory, this is certainly a welcome trend. From the practical point of view, however, it is hardly to be recommended.

Why should a game begin, as it were, with the middlegame? How can fifteen or twenty automatic book moves be considered part of a real game of chess? Yet that is exactly the situation when both players follow the "official" best line of play.

And if one of them makes an "inferior" move at

some point—what then? As my own experience
proves, these lesser-known variations can often lead
to excellent results in practical play.

The fact is, most contemporary players greatly
overestimate the importance of opening homework.
When a player works out complicated middlegame
positions with exhaustive analysis and relies too much
on opening literature, he is suppressing his creativity
in the early stages of the game. If the opening deviates
from well-known theoretical lines, he can find himself
lost in the forest. I don't think it's right for a practical
player to give up the opportunity for creative thinking
in so interesting a part of the game as the opening.

The move 3 Nc3 is an attempt to lead the game
into lesser-known paths and to force both players to
do some independent thinking from the very first
moves. I know that the theoreticians consider this
move of little interest and not dangerous for Black,
but his position is by no means without problems.

3 . . .	Nxc3
4 dxc3	d6
5 Nf3	g6

This leads to a position not entirely satisfactory for
Black. But what should he do here? In my game
against Lothar Schmid in Bamberg 1968, the German
grandmaster tried 5 . . . Nc6 6 Bb5 Bd7, but after 7
Qe2 he ran into difficulty. "Theory" gives 5 . . . dxe5
6 Qxd8+ Kxd8 7 Nxe5 Ke8 8 Bc4 e6 with equality.
Objectively, that may be correct—but who plays
Alekhine's Defense in order to switch to an endgame
before the tenth move?

6 Bc4	Nc6

Although this looks logical after White's 6 Bc4 (be-

cause now *7 Bb5* would lose an important tempo),
the immediate 6 . . . Bg7 looks better. Then 7 Ng5 e6
is not very strong for White, and 7 Bf4 0-0 enables
Black to complete his kingside development normally.

7 Bf4   e6

Of course, 7 . . . dxe5 8 Nxe5 is not pleasant for
Black, and 7 . . . Bg7 8 Ng5 0-0 9 e6 is quite annoying. The text move is proof that Black's handling of
the opening has not been flawless.

8 exd6

It was hard to make a decision here. After the game
I was inclined to prefer 8 Qe2, keeping the strongpoint e5. But the text has its good side, of course.

8 . . .   cxd6
9 Qe2   Be7

Again 9 . . . Bg7 has its drawbacks. A variation I
briefly considered during the game goes like this: 10
0-0-0 e5 11 Nxe5 (*11 Bg5* is probably even stronger)
11 . . . Nxe5 12 Bxe5 Bxe5 13 f4 0-0 14 fxe5 Qg5 +
15 Qd2! Qxd2 + 16 Rxd2 dxe5 17 Re1 with a far
superior endgame for White.

10 0-0-0   a6

White has much the better development, which fully compensates for his opponent's strongpoints in the center.

Black has some problems with his king: it will be difficult to castle queenside, and 10 ... 0-0 directly provokes a strong kingside attack starting with 11 h4. His decision to leave the king in the middle for the time being and begin an action on the queenside therefore seems correct.

11 h4   b5
12 Bb3

I was aware of the risk that this bishop might be shut out of play after ... d5, but concrete calculation revealed many dangerous tactical opportunities for White later on, mainly various sacrificial possibilities on d5. Also the move c4 could be very effective in some cases.

12 Bd3 is less obliging, but I didn't want to close the d-file.

12 ...   d5

This is the most thematic answer, though it entails great danger for Black. I expected 12 ... Na5 to eliminate my bishop, but Westerinen apparently did not want to exchange that out-of-play piece. White would probably continue 13 Qd2 d5 14 Qd4 or 14 h5, with positional pressure.

13 Rhe1!

Normally the rook would not be moved from h1, where it supports a possible kingside attack with h5, but I correctly foresaw that decisive operations would be taking place in the center. The move is directed first of all against 13 . . . Na5, which would now be met by 14 Bxd5! exd5 15 Rxd5 Bd7 16 Bc7! and wins.

Futile is 13 h5 g5, etc.

13 . . .   Bd7?

This appears at first to be a good move, preventing a later c4 and preparing an action on the queenside with . . . a5. But White refutes it combinatively by exploiting the unsafe position of Black's king. Anyway, it was not easy to see the point of White's following attack.

It's hard to suggest a good line for Black here, in view of his king's perilous position. Maybe his best practical chance is 13 . . . Ra7, again protecting his bishop on e7 against possible sacrifices on d5. But even then I would prefer White's position.

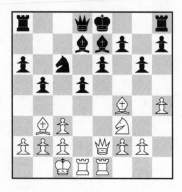

14 Bxd5!

There are two main types of sacrifices in chess. One leads to advantage through more-or-less forced variations. In the other type there are no forced variations; instead, the sacrifice is based on general considerations, on the feeling that the resulting position must be advantageous. Because the second type is more difficult to find and requires more courage, many chess critics consider that type of sacrifice the only true combination.

My sacrifice in this game lies somewhere between the two main types. It is not quite intuitive, but neither is it based completely on specific calculated variations. During the game I had the feeling that something must be happening around d5, but it was not as easy to find the concealed point then as it was later. Anyway, I felt great creative satisfaction when I found the sacrifice and its subsequent quiet point.

14 . . .   exd5
15 Ne5!

This is the move that justifies the sacrifice. A quiet move and very easy to overlook, it contains the terrible threat 16 Rxd5. The pawn cannot be protected, since 15 . . . d4 is refuted by 16 Nxc6 Bxc6 17 Rxd4 Bd7 18 Bc7!. Therefore, Black can choose between only two main defenses—the continuation in the game and 15 . . . f6, indirectly protecting the d-pawn.

When making the sacrifice I considered 15 . . . f6 and had the following long variation in mind: 16 Nxc6 Bxc6 17 Qe6! Qd7 (*17 . . . Bb7* or *17 . . . Rc8* is followed by *18 Bd6*, and after *17 . . . Bd7 18 Qxd5* is sufficient) 18 Qxf6 Rf8 19 Rxe7+! Qxe7 20 Qxc6+ Kf7 21 Qxd5+ Qe6 22 Qb7+ Kg8 (*22 . . . Qe7 23 Rd7*) 23 Bh6! Qf7 24 Rd7 and White wins. I hope it's all correct!

The obvious 15 Rxd5 leads to nothing after 15 . . . Qc8!, and now after 16 Nd4 Black has the choice between 16 . . . Be6 17 Nxe6 Qxe6 18 Qxe6 fxe6 19

Rxe6 Rc8!, or the even stronger 16 . . . 0-0! and White has no time to capture on c6 and e7.

15 . . .   Nxe5

After the game Westerinen thought of 15 . . . Qb8, with the idea 16 Nxg6 hxg6 17 Bxb8 Rxb8 18 Rxd5 Be6, or 16 Nxc6 Qxf4 + 17 Kb1 Be6!. But White plays simply 16 g3! or 16 Qf3 with a winning attack.

With the text move Black intends to return the piece and escape to an endgame with bishops of opposite colors. But since he's a pawn down with an inferior position, he has only slight drawing chances.

16 Qxe5   0-0

Black does no better with 16 . . . f6 17 Qxd5, threatening 18 Rxe7 + ! or 18 Bd6, or with 16 . . . Rf8 17 Qxd5 or 17 Rxd5, and White has two pawns and a continuing attack for his sacrificed piece.

17 Qxe7   Qxe7
18 Rxe7   Be6
19 Be5   Rfe8

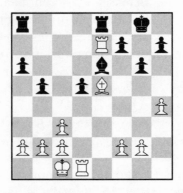

20 Rxe8 +

It often happens that, when the great complications are over and the game is entering a quiet phase, a player will miss the right continuation because he hasn't yet adjusted to the new situation. White has a very favorable endgame and all the positional trumps, and he needs only to choose a good plan to cash in his advantage. But exchanging the strong rook certainly does not make things easier. A very good continuation is 20 Rc7, and if 20 . . . Rac8 21 Rb7. By keeping the rook on the seventh rank, White retains the strong positional threat h5 followed by hxg6.

20 . . .	Rxe8
21 Bf6	h5
22 f3	Rc8
23 Kd2	Kf8
24 Re1	

I did not play this part of the game very well, though it should have been relatively easy for me to turn my advantage to account. This move, aiming to gain the initiative on the kingside, does not meet the needs of the position and only creates counterchances for my opponent. A good idea is 24 Ra1 intending a4, or simply to strengthen the position with 24 b3 followed by Ke3-d4.

24 . . .	Ke8
25 g4	hxg4
26 fxg4	Kf8!

The king returns to catch the h-pawn. Now White will have nothing but trouble with his g-pawn.

27 Rg1

Of course not 27 h5 Bxg4 28 h6 Kg8 29 h7+ Kxh7 30 Rh1+ Bh5!.

27 ...   Kg8
28 h5?

This weak move seriously jeopardizes White's advantage. The opening of the g-file gives Black's king a chance to become active by attacking the h-pawn, and it gives Black's rook a way to come into play via the open file. None of this was necessary. White still had a comfortable win by playing 28 b3 and bringing his king to d4, with various threats on the queenside.

28 ...   gxh5

Not so good is 28 ... Kh7 because of 29 h6!.

29 gxh5 +   Kh7
30 Bd4

White must take care of his h-pawn, which was threatened by 30 ... Kh6 31 Rh1 Bg4.

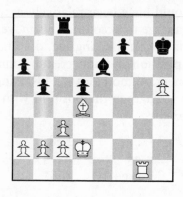

30 ...   Rg8?

A mistake, simplifying White's task. The ensuing ending is won for White despite the bishops of opposite colors because he will have passed pawns on both wings, either of which can be supported by the king.

Black's only try is 30 ... Kh6 31 Rh1 Rg8 32 Be3+ Kh7 33 Rh2. Of course White would still be much better, with a good extra pawn and chances on the queenside due to Black's many weaknesses there. But at least Black would have some active counter-play, especially with his rook, and could make White's task quite difficult.

| 31 Rxg8 | Kxg8 |
| 32 b4! | |

The key move. Now Black's weak a-pawn is fixed and cannot be protected. White can forcibly obtain the pawn formation a3-b4-c3 against Black's b5-d5, which will enable White to obtain a passed pawn on the queenside. Together with the passed pawn on the other wing, this will lead to an easily won textbook ending.

| 32 ... | Bf5 |
| 33 Be5 | Kh7 |

Bringing his king to the other side would not be of much help. White would bring his king to d4 and enter Black's camp via c5 or e5, depending on the location of Black's king. A possible variation: 33 ... Kf8 34 Ke3 Ke7 35 Kd4 Ke6 36 h6 Bxc2 37 Bf4 Bb1 (37 ... *Bh7 38 Kc5 Kf5 39 Be3 Ke4 40 Bd4* followed by *41 Kb6* doesn't help Black either) 38 Kc5 Bc2 39 Kb6 Kd7 40 Kxa6 Kc6 41 Ka5 and Black is in zugzwang: he must either allow a4 or give up his b-pawn.

34 Bf4	Bg4
35 h6	Bf5
36 Ke3	Bxc2
37 Kd4	Bb1
38 a3	

The a-pawn is needed. After 38 Kxd5? Bxa2+ 39 Kc5 Bc4 Black draws easily.

	38 . . .	Ba2
	39 Kc5	Kg6
	40 Kb6	Bc4

Black cannot stop his opponent from getting a second passed pawn. If 40 . . . Bb3 41 Kxa6 Ba4, he
loses another pawn after 42 Kb6 and 43 Kc5.

	41 Kxa6	Bd3
	42 Ka5	Kf6
	43 a4!	

Ending the game.

	43 . . .	bxa4
	44 Kxa4	Ke6
	45 Ka5	Black resigned

The white pawns win easily; e.g., 45 . . . Kd7 46 b5
Kc8 47 Kb6 f6 48 Ka7!.

This was one of my most interesting games in
Tallinn.

(September 1971)

NOT LIKE TAL
AT ALL

**Polugaevsky vs. Tal; Queen's Gambit
37th U.S.S.R. Championship, 1969**

It's an unfortunate fact that not every game between the world's best grandmasters is an uncompromising battle. That is especially true in qualification tournaments where the participants are of different classes and the top players can plan on picking up their needed points from the weaker players while treating their rivals with kid gloves. This "arithmetical" approach is one of reasons that such qualification tournaments have lost much of their appeal for the chess public.

Not quite such a simple matter was the case of the 37th U.S.S.R. Championship, which served also as a FIDE zonal tournament in the world championship cycle. Here there were only eight "weak points"; all the other fifteen players were experienced grandmasters. To attain one of the top four places and thus earn further qualification, arithmetical calculation was out of the question; it was necessary to fight hard in every game, even against one's main rivals.

Many fans expected that the game between former World Champion Tal and the current Soviet champion, Lev Polugaevsky, would be a dull draw. But the two players surprised everyone with a real fighting game, a struggle to the last move with many interesting points. It's one of the most remarkable games played in recent years.

White: Lev Polugaevsky
Black: Mikhail Tal

Queen's Gambit

1 c4	Nf6
2 Nc3	e6

It is interesting to note that the King's Indian Defense has lost much of its popularity in recent years. Tal, who used to play it in most of his games against closed openings, now usually prefers classical systems. As players' tastes change, so do opening fashions.

3 Nf3	d5
4 d4	c5

The so-called Semi-Tarrasch Defense is very popular nowadays. It leads to a certain amount of simplification with only slightly inferior chances for Black.

5 cxd5	Nxd5
6 e4	

This classical line, which was modern thirty to forty years ago, is coming back into fashion. One of the reasons may be Spassky's use of it to achieve a splendid victory in the fifth game of his 1966 world championship match with Petrosian.

6	...	Nxc3
7	bxc3	cxd4

In several games Korchnoi was successful with the new line 7 . . . Qc7. The text move is more common.

8	cxd4	Bb4+
9	Bd2	Bxd2+
10	Qxd2	0-0
11	Bc4	Nc6

Black has a choice here. With the text move he intends active counterplay on the queenside by playing . . . b6, . . . Bb7, . . . Rc8, and . . . Na5. If White remains passive, this plan will eventually give Black good prospects in the endgame after further simplification.

But things are not quite so simple. By concentrating all his pieces on the queen's wing Black leaves his king's position relatively unprotected, and White's strong center may allow him to develop a powerful attack against the enemy king. For this reason many players prefer the system 11 . . . Nd7 followed by . . . b6 and . . . Bb7, eventually developing the knight to f6.

It's hard to decide which system is best, since they both have favorable and unfavorable aspects. Ultimately the choice is a matter of taste.

12	0-0	b6
13	Rad1	

This position is not new. It was already seen in one of the games of the 1937 Alekhine–Euwe match, where Alekhine played 13 Rfd1. The question of which rook to move to d1 has been a matter of controversy. I think 13 Rad1 is more logical, allowing the other rook to go to e1 to support a later pawn advance in the center.

13 . . .   Na5

In the above-mentioned Spassky–Petrosian game, Black continued 13 . . . Bb7 14 Rfe1 Rc8 and was confronted with a tough problem after 15 d5!. He chose 15 . . . exd5 and after 16 Bxd5 got the worse game. Later analysis recommended 15 . . . Na5 instead of 15 . . . exd5, since 16 dxe6 Qxd2 17 exf7+ Kh8 seems to lead to an acceptable game for Black. After the text move, the transposition is meaningless, since after 15 . . . Na5 White can get into the present continuation with 16 Bd3!.

14 Bd3   Bb7
15 Rfe1   Rc8

This position is crucial to the evaluation of the whole variation. White, having completed his development and obtained a fine position, must now choose a plan. Up to now the usual move has been 16 Qf4, which is best answered by 16 ... Qf6, having in view a favorable endgame. But Polugaevsky comes up with a bold new idea: a surprising and interesting pawn sacrifice that also makes the game quite important theoretically.

16 d5!

Polugaevsky has been playing quickly up to this point, and since this move too was made without long deliberation, we may conclude that he had prepared the entire variation at home especially for this important tournament.

Polugaevsky later told journalists that the idea of the sacrifice had occurred to him some time before, during his joint analysis with Spassky while the latter was preparing for his world championship match with Petrosian. This shows once again how important detailed home analysis is in modern tournament play. It's hard to imagine anyone making this sacrifice over the board when facing this position for the first time—at least, not unless he was prepared to spend a lot of valuable time considering it.

16 ...   exd5

As a practical matter, Black has no choice. After 16 ... Qe7, for example, 17 Nd4! is very strong.

17 e5!

This is the point of the sacrifice. After giving up a pawn, White simply continues positionally, securing the strong central square d4 for his knight and concentrating his pieces against the enemy king. There are no direct threats: White threatens merely to strengthen his position gradually and eventually to launch a dangerous attack on the king.

As experience shows, sacrifices like this are not easy for the defender to meet. And in fact Tal does lose this game—not, however, because his position is indefensible but because in the limited time available he cannot solve the complicated problems of the defense over the board.

17 . . .   Nc4

The most likely answer, which can hardly be criticized, since the badly placed knight has to be brought back into play. It isn't easy to recommend a suitable defense for Black; in all variations White gets some kind of compensation for his pawn.

18 Qf4   Nb2?

But this is too naive. Tal must have known that the whole variation had been prepared at home. Did he think White would give up his bishop and be left after 19 Rd2 Nxd3 20 Rxd3 with practically nothing? An experienced grandmaster like Tal, who is himself ready to make all kinds of sacrifices, should have been able to calculate the results of the following sacrifice on h7.

On the other hand, we should not blame Tal too much for choosing this continuation, since he was already facing difficult problems. Maybe he would be better off with 18 . . . h6 19 Qf5 g6, and if 20 Qg4, then 20 . . . Kg7 (*21 e6 f5!*). In any case, White would still have a rather annoying initiative for the sacrificed pawn.

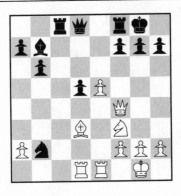

19 Bxh7 + !

The kind of typical sacrifice that was commonly seen in such positions a century ago. It doesn't happen every day that a former world champion is smashed by such a blow!

19 . . .   Kxh7
20 Ng5 +   Kg6

Obviously forced. After 20 . . . Kg8 21 Qh4 Re8 22 Qh7 + Kf8, the simplest winning line is 23 e6!.

21 h4!

With the mating threat 22 h5 + Kxh5 23 g4 + Kh6 24 Qh2 + Kg6 25 Qh7 + Kxg5 26 Qh5 + Kf4 27 Qf5 mate, which would follow 21 . . . Nxd1, for instance.

After spending an hour in thought, Tal finds the best practical chance.

21 . . .   Rc4!

Another possible defense is 21 . . . f5. Then 22 h5 + Kxh5 23 Ne6 Qe7 24 Qh2 + is not quite clear

because of 24 ... Qh4!. But White plays simply 22
Rd4! threatening 23 h5+, and on 22 ... Rh8 23 g4!
is decisive, or after 22 ... Qe7 23 Re3 Black's exposed king can hardly survive.

| 22 | h5+ | Kh6 |

Of course not 22 ... Kxh5 23 g4+! and Black gets
mated as in the previous note.

23	Nxf7+	Kh7
24	Qf5+	Kg8
25	e6!	

Now the threat is 26 e7. If 25 ... Qe7 26 h6! is
decisive, so Black's answer is forced.

25	...	Qf6
26	Qxf6	gxf6
27	Rd2!	

After all the preceding turbulence, White makes a
quiet move intending to regain his piece and go into
an endgame with an extra pawn. In view of White's
many threats, such as 28 Rxb2, 28 Nd6, 28 e7, etc.,
Black obviously can't keep his material advantage.

The question is, what's the best way to return the extra material so as to end up with a more or less acceptable position?

This is by no means an easy question, and Tal is hardly to be blamed for not finding the best answer during the game. There are many possible variations and they are all complicated; even in later analysis it was no easy matter to determine what Black should have played.

27 . . .   Rc6?

I don't think returning the piece this way is good enough for Black to save his shaky position.

An interesting line is 27 . . . Rb4, with the idea 28 e7 Kxf7, or 28 Nd6 Bc6 29 e7 Re8. But White seems to secure the advantage with 28 a3!.

Black has two main replies. 28 . . . Nc4 is met by 29 axb4 Nxd2 30 Nd6 threatening both 31 e7 and 31 Nxb7. If now 30 . . . Bc6 31 b5! and, for instance, 31 . . . Nc4 32 Nxc4 dxc4 33 bxc6 and wins. There doesn't seem to be a better defense for Black in this line.

Instead of 28 . . . Nc4 Black can play 28 . . . Rb3. A plausible line for White is 29 e7! Re8 (or 29 . . . Kxf7 30 exf8Q+ Kxf8 31 h6 and the h-pawn will cost Black a piece) 30 Nd6 Bc6 31 Nxe8 Bxe8 32 Rxd5 with clear superiority. An interesting example: 32 . . . Nd3 33 Rd8 Nxe1 34 Rxe8+ Kf7 35 h6! Rb1 36 Kh2 Rb5 37 Ra8! Kxe7 38 h7 and White wins the ending easily.

I think Black should try 27 . . . Na4. After 28 Nd6 (28 e7 Re8 29 Nd6 Bc6 leads to the same thing) 28 . . . Bc6 Black's position looks precarious, but there's no direct win for White in sight. If 29 Nxc4 dxc4

30 e7 Re8 31 Rd6 Bb5 32 Rxf6 Black gets active counterplay with 32 ... c3!. A more promising-looking line for White is 29 e7 Re8 30 Nxe8 (but not *30 Rxd5? Rxe7!*) 30 ... Bxe8 31 Rxd5 Nc5, but even here Black is by no means without chances to hold the position. Now, on the contrary, Black has to defend a very difficult endgame.

28 Rxb2   Re8

Better practical chances are offered by 28 ... Bc8, though after 29 Nh6+ Kh7 30 Nf5 Rxe6 31 Rc1! things look bad for Black. 29 ... Kh8! is a better defense, but this does not help him very much, since White can continue 30 Rbe2 Re8 31 Nf5! Rcxe6 32 Rxe6 Rxe6 (or *32 ... Bxe6 33 Nd6 Re7 34 f4*, etc.) 33 Rc1! with a position similar to the game.

29 Nh6+   Kh7
30 Nf5!

Returning the extra pawn, White builds up an easily won endgame. The knight on f5 in conjunction with the bad position of Black's king will decide.

30 ...   Rcxe6
31 Rxe6   Rxe6
32 Rc2   Rc6
33 Re2!

The decisive maneuver. Black cannot prevent the white rook's penetration to the seventh rank.

33 ...   Bc8

Tal gives the game away without a fight. He can still organize some resistance with 33 ... Rc7, stopping the lethal check on e7. White would then win a pawn with 34 Re6, but he would still have some technical problems to solve. After Tal's move the game ends quickly.

          34 Re7 +   Kh8
          35 Nh4!

Tal must have overlooked this move (time trouble?), which threatens 36 Ng6 + and 37 h6 with mate.

          35 . . .   f5
          36 Ng6 +   Kg8
          37 Rxa7   Black resigned

Polugaevsky played a fine game. Tal put up a good fight, but somewhere, unfortunately, he missed the toughest resistance. This game seems to discredit the whole variation, although only a detailed analysis of the opening can determine whether it is still playable for Black.

(December 1969)

THE GAME "UNDER" THE MOVES

Ivanovic vs. Keres; Ruy Lopez
Sarajevo 1972

One of the many attractions of chess is its variety. We see games with virtuoso attacking play, resourceful defense, profound positional maneuvering, original strategic concepts, and so on. All have one thing in common: fighting spirit. A real game of chess is impossible without the desire to fight.

In modern tournaments, unfortunately, we are witnessing a tendency toward exactly the opposite: the so-called grandmaster draw, a psuedo-fight that is justly condemned by the chess public. It is not easy to discover how the tendency developed, but it seems to me that one of its causes has been the growth of chess-playing as a profession. The traditional object of attack in a game of chess, the enemy king, has been replaced by the point.

I certainly intend no criticism of my colleagues; I

have been an offender often enough myself. But the reader may well ask why I and other grandmasters sometimes play such colorless draws. There can be many reasons: sometimes your standing in the tournament makes a draw the most sensible result; sometimes you don't feel physically ready for an all-out fight; sometimes you need an easy day in a long, exhausting tournament. Although there are many reasons for avoiding a fight, I don't think they're good enough to justify the practice.

The traditional Sarajevo tournament is known for its high number of grandmaster draws. This year's event was a refreshing exception, with only fifty percent of the games ending in draws. The tournament was a fine success for Hungary's old-timer, Laszlo Szabo, who fought here as he did in his best days.

Although my own games at Sarajevo included a few grandmaster draws, I also played some exciting fighting games, one of which I present below. Though playing a game like this is a great strain, it offers both sides considerable satisfaction.

White: B. Ivanovic
Black: Paul Keres

Ruy Lopez

1	e4	e5
2	Nf3	Nc6
3	Bb5	a6
4	Ba4	Nf6
5	0-0	Be7
6	Re1	b5
7	Bb3	0-0
8	c3	d6

9	h3	Na5
10	Bc2	c5
11	d4	Nd7

This defense first appeared in the Candidates' Tournament at Curaçao 1962, where the innovation brought me good success. By now it has been thoroughly analyzed and tested in hundreds of games. In my opinion, it is no better or worse than the usual 11 . . . Qc7.

12 Nbd2

Bobby Fischer swears by 12 dxc5 dxc5 13 Nbd2. There has not been enough practical experience with that line to come to any final conclusion, but I find it hard to believe that 11 . . . Nd7 is so inferior to 11 . . . Qc7 that Black should fear the exchange in the center. The text move is the more popular continuation.

12	. . .	cxd4
13	cxd4	Nc6

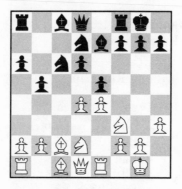

Black's strategic aim in this variation is pressure against the squares controlled by White in the center, especially d4. In some variations Black exchanges pawns there and tries to get active play for his pieces, as in the variation 14 Nf1 exd4 15 Nxd4 Nxd4 16 Qxd4 Ne5, with the possible threat 17 . . . Bxh3.

While increasing his pressure on the center, Black must always consider the possibility that White will play d5 followed by activity on the queenside. That is why most players don't continue 13 . . . Bf6 14 Nf1 Nc6, since White can then gain a tempo with 15 d5 while the bishop has nothing to do on f6.

The more popular text move intends to answer 14 Nf1 with the immediate 14 . . . exd4.

14 a4

I don't know whether this move is a novelty; I have never seen it before. The idea seems to be to force Black to play . . . b4 and thus secure the square b3 for a white knight. That would certainly be counted a success compared with 14 Nb3 at once, when Black gets counterplay with 14 . . . a5.

But compared with the usual 14 Nb3 or 14 Nf1, can 14 a4 be considered an improvement? I don't think so. First, it is a loss of time. Second—and more important—it weakens the critical b4-square, which could become a strongpoint for a black knight.

14 . . .   bxa4

It is always difficult to meet a new move over the board. I did not like 14 . . . Nxd4 15 Nxd4 exd4 very much because of 16 Nf3. Although I could find no objection to the natural 14 . . . Bb7, I chose the text move thinking it would lead to more interesting and complicated positions.

15 Bxa4   Bb7

Also possible here is 15 ... Nb4, since 16 Bxd7 Bxd7 17 dxe5 can be answered by 17 ... Nd3 (*18 exd6 Nxe1!*). And 16 Qb3 a5 17 Bxd7 Bxd7 18 dxe5 is tactically refuted by 18 ... Be6. The line 15 ... Nxd4 16 Nxd4 exd4 17 Nf3 Nc5 also looks good. The text move leads to greater complications.

16 Nc4   Qc7!

The only satisfactory defense, since 16 ... Nxd4 17 Nxd4 exd4 loses the exchange after 18 Bxd7 and 19 Nb6, and on 16 ... exd4 the exchange 17 Bxc6! Bxc6 18 Nxd4 presents Black with most unpleasant problems.

17 Ra3!?

Though White's position looks threatening, it is not easy to find a promising continuation.

On 17 d5 Nb4, the move 18 Qb3 looks very strong—but Black would not play 17 ... Nb4. Much better is 17 ... Na7! (*18 Bxd7 Qxc4!*) with a fine game.

Nor does 17 Ne3 promise very much. Black can reply 17 ... Nb6, and also 17 ... Nxd4 18 Nxd4 exd4 looks good enough.

Though the text seems attractive, it has a fundamental flaw: the rook is too exposed on a3, which enables Black to create great tactical complications.

Maybe the wisest move is 17 Bd2, giving White strong positional pressure after 17 ... Nxd4 18 Nxd4 exd4 19 Rc1 Nc5 20 Ba5 Qb8 21 Nb6 Ra7 22 Qxd4 (*22 ... Bf6 23 e5!*).

Also worth considering is 17 b3.

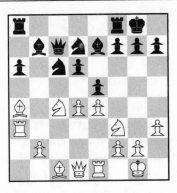

17 . . .   exd4!?

Certainly the most complicated line, but it's hard to tell, even in post-game analysis, whether the most complicated line is actually the strongest.

The first move to consider is the sharp push 17 . . . d5 18 exd5 Nxd4, but it doesn't seem to me to give White any great problems to solve. He can get an approximately equal game with 19 d6 Bxd6 20 Nxd6 Qxd6 21 Bxd7 (also good is *21 Nxd4 exd4 22 Rd3 Qd5 23 f3*) 21 . . . Bxf3 22 gxf3 Qxd7 23 Rxe5 Rad8 24 Be3. I don't see any edge for Black even after the simple 18 Rae3.

Objectively, the strongest line is probably 17 . . . Nxd4, with the idea of transposing to the line actually played after 18 Nxd4 exd4 19 Qxd4 d5!. I don't see a promising attacking continuation for White here, since Bxd7 is always met by . . . Qxd7, leaving Black without problems.

18 Bxc6!

Ivanovic fell into long thought before deciding on this exchange. I was expecting 18 Nxd4 Nxd4 19

Qxd4 d5!, and now 20 Rg3 is refuted by 20 . . . Qxg3!
21 fxg3 Bc5.

18 . . .	Bxc6
19 Nxd4	d5!

It's hard to make a decision like this when you're
over fifty. In my younger days it wouldn't have taken
me long to consider this move, but with every passing
year the variations take longer to calculate and the
possibility of error increases. And I no longer have the
ambition to fight out obscure complications.

For a long time I considered the quiet 19 . . . Nc5
but felt that White would still be better after 20 Nf5.
That may be why I returned to a combinative line and
chose the text move, which is probably Black's strongest continuation.

20 Rg3

This had to be calculated precisely, since otherwise
White remains the exchange down. After 20 exd5
Bxa3, neither 21 dxc6 Bb4 nor 21 Nxc6 Bc5 offers
White sufficient initiative for the exchange.

20 . . .	dxc4
21 Nf5	Bf6

I considered 21 . . . Nf6 22 Rxg7+ Kh8, but the
attack after 23 Qd2! would be extremely unpleasant.
After the move in the game White appears to get a
winning attack, but actually Black has a narrow, surprising way out. The game is approaching a climax.

22 Rxg7+! Bxg7

Black can play the safe 22 . . . Kh8 with a probable
draw after 23 Rxh7+ Kxh7 24 Qh5+.

23 Qg4   Qe5
24 Bh6!

Must Black resign now? There's the terrible threat of 25 Bxg7, and 24 . . . Rfe8 25 Bxg7 Qxf5 26 exf5! Rxe1+ 27 Kh2 is anything but inviting.

24 . . .   Qf6!

A most surprising defense, based on the fact that Black already has an extra rook and bishop. His position is hanging by a thread, and it's a slender one indeed!

25 Bxg7

This is the main variation, but when entering this combination Black had to analyze other possibilities. In case of 25 e5 I considered 25 . . . Qxh6 26 Nxh6+ Kh8 27 Nf5 Rg8 with pressure against g2, and 25 . . . Nxe5 26 Rxe5 Rae8! 27 Bxg7 Qg6, and Black remains a piece up.

25 . . .   Qg6
26 Ne7+

26 Bc3 Qxg4 27 Ne7 mate would be nice, but 26 ... Rfe8! leaves Black with an extra rook.

26 ...   Kxg7
27 Nxg6   hxg6
28 e5!

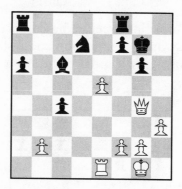

The big combinations are over and we can now examine the results. Black has a material advantage, with rook, bishop, and knight against White's queen and pawn. But White still has some attacking chances against the black king, and they should not be underestimated. Now, for instance, the threat is 29 e6, breaking up the black king's position.

28 ...   Rfe8

I did not like my position after 28 ... Bb5 29 e6 Nf6 30 Qd4 Rad8 31 Qa7, so I decided to abandon the c-pawn in order to safeguard my king. Now 29 e6 Nf6 is not dangerous for Black.

29 Qxc4   Re6

But here 29 . . . Bb5 30 Qd4 Kg8 is more precise.
Black must get his king off the dangerous diagonal as
soon as possible.

30 Qd4   Rb8

Now 30 . . . Kg8 is preferable. The rook does not
stand well on the b-file.

31 Rc1

An attempt to create a kingside attack with 31 f4
and g4 would weaken White's kingside too much.
The text move threatens 32 Rxc6, but White could
also consider 31 Re3, with the idea of an eventual
offensive on the kingside.

31 . . .   Rb7
32 b4   Nf8
33 h4   Kg8

Black has finally consolidated his position on the
kingside and can begin to think about activities on the
other side. Black's material edge should give him good
winning chances if he can avoid threats to his king.
The fact that my opponent was in serious time trouble made my job a little easier.

34 Rc5   Bd7
35 f3?

This loses the important b-pawn. White should
play 35 Qf4 to enable him to meet 35 . . . Reb6 safely
with 36 Rc4.

35 . . .   Reb6
36 Rc4   Be6

37	Rc2	Rxb4
38	Qd8	Rd7

Time trouble on both sides leads to inaccuracies. The logical line is 38 . . . Rb2, forcing White either to exchange rooks or to leave Black in possession of the second rank.

39	Qg5	Bf5

This forces White's rook to a better square. Black should use his respite from serious threats to advance his passed pawn.

40	Ra2	Rb6?

No matter how much you accomplish in a game, you can spoil much of it with one careless move, and it's often the last move before the time control. By removing the rook from its ideal position on White's fourth rank, Black gives his opponent time to begin an annoying initiative on the kingside. Naturally, 40 . . . Ne6 should be played, and if 41 Qf6 Bd3, with the threat 42 . . . Rf4.

41	h5

White sealed this obvious reply, and I left the playing room in an optimistic mood, expecting to exploit my material advantage without much trouble. But my optimism was dampened when home analysis proved that a win could be achieved only with great difficulty, if at all. The question was: Which of the many possibilities at Black's disposal offered the best practical chances?

41 ...   Rd5!?

This is probably not the strongest move, but it is certainly the one my opponent least expected. I had concluded that the obvious 41 ... Ne6 42 Qf6 Bb1 43 Ra3 gxh5 44 f4 would give White sufficient counterplay and would certainly have been thoroughly analyzed by him. The problems that arise after the move played are rather less obvious and are harder to discover without prior analysis.

42 hxg6?

Justifying my decision! This move, like 42 f4 or 42 Re2, does not create serious problems for Black. White's chances lie in 42 h6!, which creates unpleasant threats around Black's king. The point is that Black can't play 42 ... Rxe5 because of 43 Qd8!, threatening 44 h7 + .

After 42 h6 Black would still retain some winning chances with 42 ... a5 or 42 ... Re6, but the outcome would be quite unpredictable.

42 ...   Bxg6
43 f4

White had to protect his e-pawn in view of the threat 43 . . . f6.

43 . . .   Ne6
44 Qf6   Rd1 +
45 Kf2?

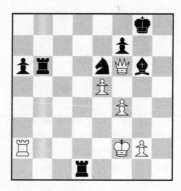

This loses at once. White should play 45 Kh2, which gives Black many crucial problems.

In my adjournment analysis I first considered 45 . . . Rbb1, with the idea 46 Rxa6 Rh1 + 47 Kg3 Rb3 + 48 Kf2 (or *48 Kg4 Bh5 + 49 Kf5 Ng7 + 50 Ke4 Bg6 +*, and now *51 Kd4 Rc1! 52 Ra8 + Kh7 53 Qh4 + Nh5*, or *51 Kd5 Rc3! 52 Ra8 + Kh7 53 Kd6 Be4*) 48 . . . Rb2 + 49 Kf3 Rf1 + 50 Kg3 Be4.

But this does not win! Instead of capturing the pawn (*46 Rxa6*), White plays 46 f5! (*46 . . . Rf1 47 Rxa6*). My first impression then was that 46 . . . Nf4 wins (*46 . . . Ng7 47 g4!*), since 47 g4 is met by 47 . . . Rd3!. But after 47 Qe7! (*47 . . . Rh1 + 48 Kg3 Nh5 + 49 Kg4!*, or *47 . . . Nh5 48 g4!*), I could not find a promising line for Black. So I had to abandon 45 . . . Rbb1.

My next try was 45 ... Rf1, which must be answered by 46 Ra4. Now 46 ... Bd3 looks very strong, but White has the surprising resource 47 f5!. If now 47 ... Bxf5?, then 48 Rh4! wins, since both Black pieces are pinned. And after 47 ... Rxf5 48 Rg4+ Kf8 49 Qh8+ Ke7 50 Qh4+, White has various tactical chances. This line, too, is unsatisfactory for Black.

Finally, I returned to 45 ... Rf1 46 Ra4 Rbb1!. After 47 Rxa6 Rh1+ 48 Kg3 Rb3+, this leads to a position discussed earlier. But here again White has a better move in 47 Rc4!. Still, I decided this was the best variation for Black in view of the possibility 47 ... Rh1+ 48 Kg3 Ng7! 49 Qd8+ Kh7 50 Rc8 Rb3+ 51 Kf2 Rb2+ 52 Kg3 (52 Ke3 Re1+, or 52 Kf3 Bh5+! 53 g4 Rh3+ 54 Ke4 Re2+) 52 ... Nf5+ 53 Kg4 (53 ... Kf3 54 Nh4+ 54 Ke3 Re1+) 53 ... Rxg2+ 54 Kf3 Nh4+, and White will lose his queen.

45 ...   Bb1!

The simplest. Now Black gains control of his seventh rank, since 46 Re2 loses the f-pawn after 46 ... Bd3 (47 f5 Bxe2 48 Kxe2 Nf4+!).

46 Ra4   Rb2+
47 Kg3   Rg1

Winning the g-pawn, which means the end. White can't play 48 Rxa6 because of 48 ... Be4!.

48 Rc4   Rgxg2+
49 Kh3

Or 49 Kf3 Ng5 + ! 50 Ke3 Rg3 + 51 Kd4 Ne6 + 52 Kd5 Ba2 and wins.

$$49 \ldots \qquad \text{Rg6?}$$

We live and learn! Despite my forty years of tournament experience, I still break elementary rules of the game.

The rule in this case says that you should never look for other possibilities when you have found one satisfactory winning line. I saw that Black wins comfortably with 49 ... Ng5 + ! 50 fxg5 (or *50 Kh4 Rh2 +* with a mate) 50 ... Rh2 + 51 Kg3 Rbg2 + 52 Kf3 Rf2 + 53 Kg3 Rxf6 54 Rc8 + Kh7, remaining a piece ahead. But then I got the idea that the text move wins even more efficiently—a careless idea for which I was very nearly punished.

50 Rc8 +	Nf8
51 Rxf8 +	

I had seen that 51 e6 Rxf6 52 e7 fails to 52 ... Bf5 + .

51 ...	Kxf8
52 Qh8 +	Ke7
53 Qc8!	

But I had completely overlooked this simple move, protecting the critical f5-square. Now White threatens not only 54 Qc5 + but also 54 f5—and the flag on my clock was approaching the time control. To gain time, I gave a few checks.

53 ...	Rh6 +
54 Kg4	Rg6 +
55 Kh3	

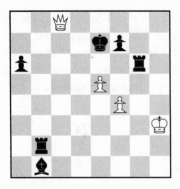

A better chance is 55 Kf3, although it would not have been adequate to save the game, as later analysis proved. Black would win with 55 ... R2b6! 56 f5 Bxf5 57 Qxf5 Rgf6!, or 56 Qc5+ Kd7 57 Qd5+ Ke8 58 Qa8+ Ke7, etc. But that line still had to be found!

55 ...	Rb3+
56 Kh4	

And here 56 Kh2 was more stubborn. Black again answers 56 ... R3b6! and if 57 f5 Bxf5 58 Qxf5 Rh6+ 59 Kg3 Rbg6+ followed by 60 ... Rf6!, etc.

56 ...	Rh6+
57 Kg4	Rg6+
58 Kh4	Bf5!

A nice finish. The bishop must be taken, since 59 Qc5+ or 59 Qc7+ is met by 59 ... Ke8 and White has no more checks.

59 Qxf5	Rb8
White resigned	

The only defense against 60 ... Rh8+ is 60 Qh5, but then 60 ... Rg1! wins the queen.

This was a really full fighting game that I enjoyed very much and hope you enjoyed too. But fifteen games like this in a single tournament—I don't think I could stand it! So please, have a little understanding for my next grandmaster draw. . . .

(July 1972)

TAL
WINS A DRAW

Mukhin vs. Tal; Nimzo-Indian Defense
U.S.S.R. Team Championship, 1972

In the spring of 1972, Moscow welcomed all the best chess players in the U.S.S.R. for the final matches of the national team championship. The finals comprised seventeen teams from all the Soviet republics and the cities of Moscow and Leningrad. Each team consisted of five men, two women, three boys, and two girls. With twenty-two grandmasters and eighty-three masters, plus many others, this was the biggest Soviet chess event in many years. It was won by the Moscow team, led by former World Champion Tigran Petrosian.

With so many experts, the championship naturally produced a great many interesting games. One of the most instructive was the Mukhin–Tal game, which was played in one of the preliminary groups.

For years the chess world has been suffering from a

worsening illness—the so-called grandmaster draw (though I'm not sure that name is valid, since it isn't necessary to be a grandmaster to produce a dull, short draw). What is the remedy?

It is no easy matter to enforce a universal cure for this problem, so it is up to each player to fight for himself. Obviously, it requires the cooperation of both players to produce such a draw. If one of them decides to fight, even the dullest position can offer possibilities to the creative mind.

The following game confirms that assumption. When playing against Tal—virtually the personification of vigorous, combinative chess—inexperienced masters usually tend to avoid complications and head for simplification. In this game, indeed, White achieves a totally drawish position without queens and an almost symmetrical position—just the kind of position in which you would expect to see a handshake and a quick draw.

Yet even in such a dead-draw position, Tal manages to find ways to create complications. Suddenly White is confronted with problems, and the result is a fine, interesting game that would be a credit to any tournament.

White: M. Mukhin
Black: Mikhail Tal

Nimzo-Indian Defense

1	d4	Nf6
2	c4	e6
3	Nc3	Bb4
4	e3	

When I was a young player, almost everybody

chose 4 Qc2. Today's fashion is 4 e3 to the exclusion of almost everything else.

                4 ...   0-0
                5 Ne2

Most players prefer 5 Bd3 and 6 Nf3, which in my opinion is a more natural choice. The text is not bad if Black answers 5 ... c5, but now, when Black can play 5 ... d5, White's move is not very effective.

                5 ...   d5
                6 a3   Be7

Some masters even prefer 6 ... Bd6, willing to sacrifice a tempo to lure White into playing c5. But the normal text move seems good enough.

                7 Nf4

White has a decision to make here. If he refrains from exchanging pawns, he must consider the possible counterplay resulting from ... dxc4 followed by ... c5. In that case, White wants a knight on f3, where it protects the important center square d4. For instance, after 7 Ng3 dxc4 8 Bxc4 c5, Black certainly has no problems in the opening.

The other choice is 7 dxc5. That looks more logical to me, since after g3 and Bg2 White's pieces are developed normally.

The knight is badly posted on f4 and enables Black to get comfortable equality.

                7 ...   c6

Here, too, 7 ... dxc4 and 8 ... c5 is playable. But Tal is fond of the position after 8 cxd5 exd5, which leads to a middlegame with chances for both sides.

     8   Bd3   dxc4
     9   Bxc4   Nbd7

This threatens 10 . . . e5, which would relieve Black of all his remaining opening problems.

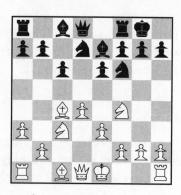

           10   Nd3

Tal thought 10 Bxe6!? was better, but I can't agree. As we will see, the text move is good enough for equality. But the complications after 10 Bxe6 fxe6 11 Nxe6 Qe8 12 Nxf8 (or *12 Nc7 Qg6 13 Nxa8 Qxg2*) 12 . . . Nxf8 13 0-0 Bd6 offer White nothing more than difficult chances to equalize. Black's pieces would be well developed and directed toward the white king's position, while White would have only theoretical chances to advance his pawn majority on the queenside. I would prefer the Black position.

           10 . . .   c5

This leads to full equality and an almost symmetrical structure in which a draw would be the most likely result. If Black wants a more complicated middlegame, he can try 10 . . . Qc7 first, with an eye toward . . . e5.

11	dxc5	Nxc5
12	Nxc5	Bxc5
13	Qxd8	

White shows no ambition to achieve anything in the opening. With 13 Qe2 he can get a normal middlegame with a full game in store.

13	...	Rxd8
14	b4	Be7

What can be expected from this position other than a divided point? Objectively, it is certainly drawish. White needs only to play 14 Ke2 followed by 15 Rd1 with further simplification to follow. Then even Tal could hardly avoid splitting the point.

But White seems to have convinced himself that the game will be drawn all by itself. His last move was not a gain of a tempo but a weakening of White's position on the c-file, and his later careless play will give him new problems. It isn't long before we find, rather surprisingly, that his position has become indefensible.

Even drawish positions must be played with care when Tal is your opponent!

15 Bb2   Bd7
16 Ke2

According to general principles, this is a good move, since in the endgame the king should remain in the center. But in this case Tal disagrees. According to him, the endgame is still a long way off, and in the coming middlegame the king may be too exposed in the center. The text move does not by itself place White in serious difficulties, but 16 0-0 would be more prudent.

16 ...   Rac8
17 Bd3

White is beginning to feel a little uncomfortable. His move leads to a dangerous initiative for Black, but he would have problems also after 17 Bb3 Bc6 18 f3 Nd5!.

17 ...   Bc6
18 f3   Nd7!

This must have come as a surprise to White. The move is tactically justified, since 19 b5 leads to a clear advantage for Black after 19 ... Ne5 20 bxc6 Nxd3 21 cxb7 Rb8.

Black's threat of 19 ... Ne5 is not easy to handle.

19 Ne4   f5!

Tal points out that 19 ... Bb5 20 Bxb5 Rc2+ leads to nothing because of 21 Nd2 Rxb2 22 Rac1 with further simplification.

20 Nd2?

It was not easy to foresee that this natural-looking move would turn out to be a decisive mistake. In spite of all his previous inaccuracies, White can still get a playable game with 20 Nf2!, protecting the bishop on d3. But after this positional error, he will soon have a lost game.

20 ...   Nb6!

After this simple move, White has no adequate defense against the terrible threat 21 ... Rxd3! followed by 22 ... Bb5 +. All it took were a few careless moves to change a drawn position into a lost one!

21 Bd4

White hopes to avoid the main threat by closing the d-file, but it doesn't work. Other continuations offer no better chances; for instance, 21 b5 Rxd3! 22 bxc6 Rcd8 23 Bd4 Rxd2 + ! 24 Kxd2 e5 25 cxb7 (or *25 c7 Rd7 26 Rac1 Nc8*, etc.) 25 ... exd4, and Black's two pieces are much stronger than White's rook. On 21 Nb3, Black still plays 21 ... Rxd3! 22 Kxd3 Bb5 + 23 Kd2 Nc4 +, with a decisive attack.

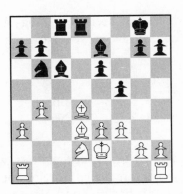

21 ...   e5!

Renewing the threat . . . Rxd3 by removing the bishop from d4. It's amazing how strong an attack Black has been able to develop from that relatively simple queenless position.

22 Bc5

In this way White hopes to bring his king to safety across the c-file, but it costs him a lot of material. Clearly, 22 Bxb6 is also met by 22 . . . Rxd3!, and 22 Bxe5 Rxd3! 23 Kxd3 Bb5+ 24 Kd4 Na4 draws the white king into a mating net. During the game, Tal couldn't find an immediate mate after 25 Kd5, though he knew that White must be lost with his king so exposed. Later he demonstrated the following forced mate: 25 . . . Kf7 26 Bd4 Bf6! 27 Bxf6 gxf6 28 Kd6 Rc6+ 29 Kd5! Rc7 30 Ne4 Rd7+ 31 Nd6+ Ke7 and mate next move.

22 . . .   Rxd3!

This sacrifice has been following White like a plague for the last few moves. Now it's decisive for Black.

        23 Kxd3   Bb5+
        24 Kc2   Na4!

The coordinated black attack runs wonderfully. Now 25 . . . b6 is threatened, forcing the white king off the c-file. But it has no good place to go.

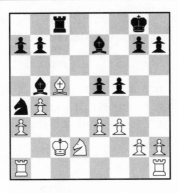

25 Kb3

The most plausible retreat is 25 Kd1, but then 25
. . . Bf6! renews the threat 26 . . . b6 with lethal effect;
for instance, 26 e4 (*26 . . . e4* was also threatened) 26
. . . b6 27 Be3 Rc3 28 Bf2 (*28 Re1 Nb2* would be a
noteworthy mate!) 28 . . . Nb2+ 29 Ke1 Bg5, and
White can't avoid further loss of material.

25 Kb1 is also met by 25 . . . b6!; e.g., 26 Bxe7
Bd3+ 27 Ka2 Rc2+ 28 Kb3 Rb2+! 29 Kxa4 a6,
and there is no defense against 30 . . . Bb5 mate. Wonderful variations!

25 . . .   b6

A few moves earlier White suffered under the fatal
threat of . . . Rxd3; now it is this move. There is no
reasonable defense.

26 Nc4

The main variation is 26 Bxe7 Rc3+ 27 Ka2 Rc2+
28 Kb1 (or *28 Kb3 Rb2* mate!) 28 . . . Bd3!, threatening 29 . . . Nc3 mate. With the move played, White

offers to give up some material to repulse the attack, but it only postpones the inevitable.

26 ...   bxc5

Black has regained his sacrificed material and ended up with a decisive material advantage: two bishops against a rook. And the attack still rages.

27 Nxe5   cxb4
28 Rac1

White can't allow 28 ... Rc3 + .

28 ...   Nc5 +
29 Kxb4   a6!

Even stronger than the immediate 29 ... Nd3 + . Since White must now lose more material, he resigned.

It is games like this that make chess so attractive to most of us!

(October 1972)

GAME 11

IF YOU SAY "OOPS,"
TAL SAYS "MATE"

Tal vs. Keres; Ruy Lopez
Tallinn 1973

The traditional Tallinn International Tournament is one of those "chess for fun" tournaments in which everyone can play freely and creatively without having to worry about getting enough points to earn an international title or to qualify for some other event. This kind of tournament produces interesting games that are fun for all. I know I speak for most of the participants in this year's tournament when I say that we enjoyed one another's fighting spirit and the many beautiful games that resulted.

This year's event brought together a number of fine players. Boris Spassky was making his first appearance after his world championship match against Fischer, and everyone was interested in seeing how he would perform. Another former world champion, Mikhail Tal, had just won the championship of the

U.S.S.R. as well as the strong Wijk aan Zee tournament in Holland. Grandmaster Polugaevsky is regularly included among the highest-rated players in the world. And when you have David Bronstein among the participants you know you can count on at least several exciting games full of original ideas.

The young grandmaster Yuri Balashov, who had done very well at Wijk aan Zee, was here to prove that his result there had not been a fluke. The tournament also included Ulf Andersson, the promising young grandmaster from Sweden; Jan Timman, the Dutch junior hopeful; Helmut Pfleger, a member of the successful German team at the Skopje Olympiad; and Pribyl from Czechoslovakia and Popov from Bulgaria.

Anthony Saidy from the U.S. and Heikki Westerinen from Finland came to try to improve on their results in the 1971 event, and with four players from Estonia, who in most cases offered worthy opposition, we had a competition with sixteen strong players.

The main interest was focused on the two former world champions. Tal, having been in the lead from the first rounds, won the tournament cleanly. This was a fine victory for him, and, with his two previous first places, he has now run up a string of more than eighty games without a loss. He seems to have regained his top form of the 1960s, though he now conducts his games on a more solid positional basis. I wonder what he will show in the upcoming world championship cycle.

Spassky did not do as well as his many admirers expected, but there may have been good reasons for that. Since the Alekhine Memorial Tournament in Moscow 1971, Spassky had played only the match with Fischer, so it is understandable that he may not have been in top form. Also, this was one of those relaxing events in which one could experiment and not worry about one's place in the final crosstable. It will take much more practical play for Spassky to return to his usual form.

It was not easy to choose only one of the tournament's many fighting games. Finally I decided to give you a demonstration of the present state of former World Champion Tal's wonderful talent.

White: Mikhail Tal
Black: Paul Keres

Ruy Lopez

1	e4	e5
2	Nf3	Nc6
3	Bb5	a6
4	Ba4	d6

Although this is certainly one of the most solid lines of play against the Ruy Lopez, it is more passive than the usual 4 . . . Nf6.

5 0-0

Years ago this was considered not best in view of 5 . . . Bg4 6 h3 h5, but since we now know that that line is rather risky for Black, 5 0-0 has become White's most popular choice.

Although theory considers 5 Bxc6+ bxc6 6 d4 very good for White, that system is rarely used in practice.

5 . . .	Bd7
6 c3	

The immediate 6 d4 is considered best, since 6 . . .
b5 7 Bb3 Nxd4 8 Nxd4 exd4 9 c3 gives White a
strong initiative for the pawn. Now Black can choose
a system in which White's 5 0-0 may turn out to have
been a bit premature.

$$6 \ldots \qquad \text{Nge7}$$
$$7 \text{ d4} \qquad \text{Ng6}$$

It seems to me that Black has solved his opening
problems satisfactorily and now stands quite well.

$$8 \text{ Re1} \qquad \text{Be7}$$
$$9 \text{ Nbd2} \qquad \text{h6!}$$

A well-known method of exchanging the dark-
squared bishop, which somewhat relieves Black's
cramped position and is positionally well justified. Of
course, 9 . . . 0-0 is good, too.

$$10 \text{ Nf1} \qquad \text{Bg5}$$
$$11 \text{ Be3}$$

The point is that White cannot exchange on g5
without giving his opponent excellent attacking
chances on the h-file. On the other hand, after 11 Ne3
Bxe3 12 Bxe3 0-0, White will miss his knight, which
was on its way to d5, and his bishop pair will be of
little practical value.

With the text move White offers to trade bishops so
as to keep his good knight on e3. Black does him that
favor, but keeping the tension with 11 . . . Qf6 is also
good.

$$11 \ldots \qquad \text{Bxe3}$$
$$12 \text{ Nxe3} \qquad \text{0-0}$$

The game is about even. White has some advantage

in space, but Black's position is without weaknesses and his pieces are well placed.

13 Bc2   Re8

The most logical course here is 13 . . . Nh4 to force further simplification. But on the spur of the moment I decided to keep the tension and not exchange my well-posted knight on g6. An old chess adage advises, however, that cramped positions should be eased by exchanges, if possible.

14 Qd2   Rc8
15 g3

Tal is always on the lookout for ways to keep the position under tension, even at the cost of creating minor weaknesses. Here he prevents 15 . . . Nh4, which would have led to full equality after, for instance, 15 Rad1, and he also keeps his opponent's knight out of the strong square f4. Certainly it will be hard for Black to exploit the slight weakening of White's king's position, but not everyone would risk playing 15 g3.

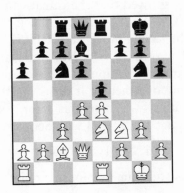

15 . . .   Qf6

I know Tal well enough to assume that he did not intend to protect his knight with 16 Qd1 but was more likely to play the variation 16 Kg2 Bh3+ 17 Kxh3 Qxf3 18 Nd5, threatening to trap the queen with 19 Bd1. Then 18 . . . Nh4?! 19 Kxh4 Qg2 hardly gives Black sufficient attacking chances; for instance, after 20 Ne3 Qxh2+ 21 Kg4 the king escapes via f3. But 18 . . . Qh5+ 19 Kg2 Qg5! suffices to get an equal game.

The most likely idea, however, was 16 Nd5, planning to trap the queen after 16 . . . Qxf3 17 Bd1. But is the queen really trapped? Black has the resource 17 . . . Nh4!, threatening mate on g2, and after 18 gxh4 Qh3 the queen is saved.

Having satisfied myself on that score, I began to study the position after 18 . . . Qh3. Unless White had some way to force an advantage, he would stand worse in view of his weakened pawn position. What could he do?

Looking more deeply into the position, I found the surprising 19 Nf6+! gxf6 20 Qxh6, threatening 21 Re3 with an immediate win. Is Black lost? No! Further analysis showed that the threat can be repulsed by 20 . . . exd4 21 cxd4 Nxd4, and if now 22 Re3, Black has the saving move 22 . . . Nf5!.

And so I played 15 . . . Qf6. But I am forced to admit that my calculation of the variations was far inferior to my opponent's. It turns out that my play for complications was a serious error. I should have played the quiet 15 . . . Bh3 with about even chances.

16 Nd5!   Qxf3

There was still time to choose a quiet line with 16 . . . Qd8 or even 16 . . . Qe6, but I was curious to see what my opponent had in mind.

17 Bd1   Nh4
18 gxh4   Qh3
19 Nf6 + !

Anyway! Now I began to recheck the variations I had calculated, and I soon found the hole: After 19 ... gxf6 20 Qxh6 exd4 White need not use e3 to transfer his rook to the g-file but can accomplish that with 21 Kh1! threatening 22 Rg1 + .

Can Black afford to enter that line or not? The calculations began again.

Position after 21 Kh1 (analysis)

Apparently, 21 . . . Bf5 22 Rg1+ Bg6 will not do because of 23 Rxg6+ fxg6 24 Qxg6+ Kf8 25 Qxf6+ Kg8 26 Bb3+ Kh7 27 Qf7+ Kh6 28 Rg1 and wins. Another try, 21 . . . Rxe4, doesn't work either: 22 Rg1+ Bg4 23 Bxg4 (*23 f3 Re1!*) 23 . . . Rxg4 24 Rxg4+ Qxg4 25 Rg1 with good winning chances. There remains only 21 . . . Ne5! 22 Rg1+ Bg4 (*22 . . . Ng4 23 Bxg4 Bxg4 24 Rg3!*), and after 23 cxd4 I considered Black's position lost, since I saw no defense against 24 dxe5.

But the defense is quite simple: 23 . . . Nf3!. I completely overlooked this move, which gives White difficult problems. It threatens mate on h2, and if 24 Qf4 then 24 . . . Kf8! (but not *24 . . . Rxe4 25 Qxf3!*), and White can't take either way on g4. If White tries 24 Rg2, 24 . . . Rxe4 is good enough to give Black a clear advantage.

Does White have anything better than 23 cxd4, or is his sacrifice unsound? An attempt like 23 Qf4 is not dangerous, since Black can play 23 . . . Kf8 24 Bxg4 Qxh4 with the better game. Also, 23 Rg2 is anything but strong, since Black has the simple 23 . . . dxc3 (*24 bxc3 Qxc3*).

Therefore, White's most reasonable solution is 23 Rg3, which leads after 23 . . . Qf1+ 24 Rg1 Qh3 to a repetition of moves and a draw. Somebody once told me that chess is, after all, a deadly drawish game!

Having overlooked the rejoinder 23 . . . Nf3! I decided to decline the sacrifice, figuring that although I was giving up the exchange my position was far from lost.

19 . . .	Kh8?
20 Nxe8	Rxe8
21 h5	

Black has good compensation for the exchange. First, White must lose a pawn. Second, the position of White's king is quite unsafe. Having spent a lot of energy calculating the previous complicated variations, I was worried about the approaching time trouble and decided to play a simple line. Objectively, the sharp 21 ... f5! (22 exf5 Rf8) is correct here, to take advantage of White's exposed king. I don't think White could then have capitalized on his slight material advantage.

21 ...	Bg4
22 Qe3	Qxh5
23 Kh1	Bxd1

From here on I made my opponent's task easy. Much better is 23 ... Ne7 followed by 24 ... Ng6.

| 24 Raxd1 | Qh4 |

And here 24 ... exd4 25 cxd4 f5 should be considered.

25 Qf3	Kg8
26 Re3	Rf8
27 Qg3	Qe7

Again imprecise. Necessary is 27 ... Qf6 first, and then 28 Rf3 Qe7. By achieving the advance f4 White increases his advantage.

| 28 f4! | exf4 |

Maybe 28 ... f5 29 exf5 Rxf5 is a better try.

29 Qxf4	Re8
30 Rg1	Kh7
31 Rg4	Nd8

A good defending move is 31 ... Qf8, keeping an

eye on the possibility of playing ... Ne7. The text move allows White to make further progress.

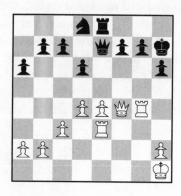

32 e5!   d5?

The threat was 33 exd6 Qxe3 34 Qxe3 Rxe3 35 dxc7. Black loses material after 32 ... dxe5 33 Rxe5 followed by 34 Qe4+, but 32 ... Qf8! is much better: after 33 exd6 Rxe3 34 Qxe3 Qxd6 White would still have a lot of technical work to do.

But now White will get the square f6 for his rook, which considerably strengthens his attack.

33 Rh3   Qf8

Of course not 33 ... Nd6? 34 Rxg7+!.

34 Rf3   Kh8
35 Qf5   Qe7

35 ... Re6 offers better chances.

36 b4   Rf8
37 Qh5   Ne6?

The decisive mistake. Black's position is difficult, but he should still try 37 ... Re8 (*38 Rf6 Qf8!*). Now Black loses by force.

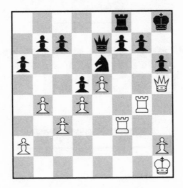

| 38 | Rf6! | Kh7 |
| 39 | Qf5 + | Kh8 |

Or 39 ... g6 40 Rgxg6! fxg6 41 Qxg6 + Kh8 42 Qxh6 + Kg8 43 Rxe6.

| 40 | Qh5 | Kh7 |
| 41 | Rh4! | Kg8 |

The time pressure is over and the game was adjourned here. Good enough to win is 42 Rxh6 gxh6 43 Qxh6 Qxh4 (43 ... f5 44 exf6!) 44 Qxh4, etc. Tal finds an even more decisive way.

| 42 | Qg4! | Ng5 |

After 42 ... Kh7 43 Qh3! the decisive sacrifice on h6 can no longer be prevented.

| 43 | Rhxh6! | Ne4 |

Also hopeless is 43 ... gxh6 44 h4, etc.

| 44 | Qh5! | gxh6 |
| 45 | Rxh6 | Black resigned |

A loss like this is nothing to be ashamed of, and winning it must have been very satisfying for Tal.

(June 1973)

IT'S ONLY A HORSE, OF COURSE . . .

Keres vs. Westerinen; Pirc Defense
Tallinn 1973

Years ago, when opening theory was made up of separate, clearly defined variations that had been played in actual games and evaluated by leading experts, a player prepared an opening by choosing a variation, verifying its soundness, and then looking for improvements. This did not involve a great deal of work.

The situation is somewhat different today, and preparing for tournament play has become a much bigger job. Nowadays we must deal not merely with individual variations but with entire systems, many of them based not only on practical experience but also on exhaustive home analysis. We know of players who have tested certain critical positions in dozens and even hundreds of speed games so that during tournament play they will feel completely at home no matter what course the opening might take.

Is it better to study individual variations or whole systems? I am inclined to think that the latter produces better practical results. Although it is hardly possible to consider every conceivable detail of every variation, studying an entire system gives the player a better feel for the entire range of possible positions. Studying individual variations, on the other hand, enables the player to produce more precise analysis.

Although I am reluctant to recommend one method over the other, I should point out that the modern attitude of system-analysis involves certain risks. In the following game from the Tallinn International Tournament, Westerinen, playing Black, chooses the currently very popular Pirc-Ufimtsev Defense. His opening strategy is basically sound, as hundreds of games have proved, yet he suffers a terrible debacle. Why? Because his method was tactically defective.

Sound principles must always be obeyed in chess, but you can't allow your opponent to destroy your plans by tactical means.

White: Paul Keres
Black: Heikki Westerinen

Pirc-Ufimtsev Defense

1	d4	g6
2	e4	Bg7
3	Nc3	d6
4	Bg5!?	

The "normal" moves in this position are 4 Nf3 and 4 f4, either of which leads to well-known, deeply analyzed positions. With the text move White tries to intimidate his opponent into not playing 4 ... Nf6 because of 5 e5, at the same time hoping to entice him to play the "standard" move 4 . . . c5. Such combining of themes from different variations often leads to surprising success, as here.

4 . . .   c5?

Everyone "knows" that the correct response to Bg5 is . . . c5. That is correct in principle, but here it is refuted by tactical means that were not foreseen by Black. Westerinen had apparently made a study of this system in a general way but without deeper analysis of specific variations.

Nothing is wrong with the "normal" 4 . . . Nf6. The only move Black has to fear is 5 e5, but then theory recommends 5 . . . dxe5 (after 5 . . . Nfd7 6 f4 f6 7 exf6 exf6 8 Bh4 White gets a slightly better game) 6 dxe5 Ng4 (6 . . . Qxd1+ 7 Rxd1 Nfd7 8 Nd5 Bxe5 9 Nf3 Bd6 10 Bxe7! leads to difficulties for Black) 7 Qxd8+ Kxd8 8 Rd1+ Bd7 9 f4. Vasja Pirc (one of the inventors of this opening) now continues 9 . . . h6! 10 Bh4 g5 with a good game for Black.

It is quite possible that the above variations can be strengthened for White. In any case they may not be to everyone's taste. If Black prefers a safer line, the immediate 4 . . . h6 can be recommended.

5 dxc5   Qa5

The idea of 4 . . . c5 was certainly not to get a clearly inferior position now with 5 . . . dxc5 6 Qxd8+ Kxd8 7 0-0-0+, etc.

6 Qd2   Qxc5

Again quite normal. If Black had foreseen all the difficulties in store for him he probably would have preferred 6 . . . Bxc3, although the position would have remained clearly in White's favor after, e.g., 7 bxc3 Qxc5 8 Qd4.

7 Nd5!

This strong move is strategically decisive. Now the normal coordination of the black pieces will be destroyed and he will be unable to organize effective counterplay.

Of course, the pawn cannot be taken: if 7 ... Bxb2 8 Rb1 threatening both 9 Rxb2 and 9 Be3. But otherwise Black must do something about the threatened loss of his queen after 8 Be3 Qc6 9 Bb5!.

$$7 \dots \qquad Be6$$
$$8 \ c4$$

White decides to strengthen the vital strongpoint for his knight on d5 and to continue in positional style. But more active continuations are possible. One promising line is 8 Bb5 + ! Nd7 9 c4, after which Black can't play 9 ... a6 because of 10 Be3 Qc8 11 Nb6, etc.

$$8 \dots \qquad Nd7$$
$$9 \ Rc1 \qquad Ngf6$$
$$10 \ f3 \qquad a5$$

Black has completed the formal development of his pieces, even outdistancing his opponent in this respect. But as we all know, to move a piece is not necessarily to develop it properly. This is a typical case. Black has brought all his pieces out, but obviously to the wrong squares. His queen is badly placed and so is his bishop on e6. Castling on either side is impossible, and any exchange on d5 would improve White's position after cxd5.

Under such circumstances it is not easy to recommend a good plan for Black. His intention, as his last move indicates, is to simplify the position somewhat after 11 Ne2 Bxd5 12 cxd5 Qb4, but even that would leave White with a clear positional advantage after, for instance, 13 Nc3 or 13 Nd4.

11 Be3

Black's last move weakened the square b5, where White now plans to bring his knight from the kingside. This move also avoids Black's intended simplification.

11 ...	Qc8	
12 Ne2	Qb8	

Black wants to play ... Nc5 but must move the queen first to avoid the threat Nb6. Maybe 12 ... Qd8 is better, protecting the e-pawn in preparation for castling and also controlling the b6-square against a possible incursion by the white knight. In either case, it is no pleasure for Black to have to play a position like this.

13 Nd4	Nc5
14 Nb5	

Now the threat of 15 Nbc7+ is hard to meet, so Black is practically forced to exchange on d5.

14 . . .   Nxd5

Although Black is already lost strategically, after this exchange White can increase his advantage by means of a nice tactical finesse. The only way to offer any resistance is 14 . . . Bxd5 15 cxd5 Nfd7, although even that leaves White with a big positional plus after 16 Be2 and 17 0-0.

15 cxd5   Bd7

Westerinen's strategy may be questionable some-times, but his tactical ability is usually on a high level. Here he offers a pawn so that after 16 Bxc5 dxc5 17 Rxc5 0-0 he would get good counterplay on the dark squares. That probably would not compensate for his material deficit, but it would give him a slight initiative and at least *some* counterplay. Naturally, White is not willing to give up his fine position for so slight a material gain.

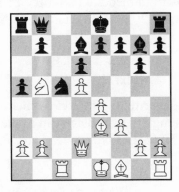

16 Rxc5!

According to an old maxim, solid positional play often leads to situations in which an advantage can be increased by tactical or sacrificial means. White offers the exchange to keep the enemy king in the center, where it will be exposed to a dangerous attack.

White also considered the simple 16 Bxc5 dxc5 17 d6 but rejected it because of 17 . . . exd6 18 Nxd6 + Ke7 (*19 Nxf7 Rf8*), and the black pieces are coordinated for counterplay. The text continuation relies on the fact that White's bishop is much stronger than the rook in this position.

16 . . .	dxc5
17 d6!	exd6

There seems to be no good defense. After 17 . . . e6, White carries out the threat 18 Nc7 + followed by 19 Nxa8 and 20 Bxc5 with a solid extra pawn. Also hopeless is 17 . . . Bxb5 18 Bxb5 + Kf8 19 dxe7 + Kxe7 20 Bxc5 +, etc., as well as 17 . . . 0-0 18 dxe7 Re8 19 Qxd7.

At first glance, 17 . . . b6 looks reasonable, but it actually leads to immediate loss after 18 Nc7 + Kd8 19 dxe7 + ! Kxe7 20 Bf4! threatening 21 Nd5 + or 21 Qd6 +.

18 Nxd6 +	Kf8
19 Nxf7!	

This is stronger than 19 Bxc5, which would have been good enough to win. Black can't take the knight, since 19 . . . Kxf7 20 Qxd7 + leads to mate.

19 . . .	Be6

This is the move Westerinen was relying on. His intention was to answer 20 Nxh8 with 20 . . . Qe5!, getting active counterplay in exchange for a pawn or two. But I did not sacrifice the exchange in order to break my own attack by capturing an undeveloped rook on h8!

20 Ng5!

It is Black's king that White is after. Now Black has little choice, since 20 . . . Qe5 loses at once after 21 Bxc5 + Kg8 22 Nxe6 Qxe6 23 Qc2, with the terrible threat 24 Bc4.

20 . . .	Bxa2
21 Bxc5 +	Kg8
22 b4	

The winning attack. A hundred years ago many players might have overlooked the point: 22 . . . axb4 23 Qxa2 + ! Rxa2 24 Bc4 mate. But in the twentieth century . . .

22 . . .	Bb3
23 Qd3	

A slight slip. The beautiful move 23 Qc2! would have shortened the game by a few moves: 23 . . . a4 24 Qxb3 + !, or 23 . . . Bf7 24 Bc4.

	23 ...	Bf7
	24 Nxf7	

Now this direct move is necessary to win the game, since 24 Qc4 Qf4 25 Nxf7 Qxf7 26 Qc2 allows the escape 26 ... axb4! 27 Bc4 Bc3 + !.

	24 ...	Qf4
	25 Ng5!	

Again the rook is ignored in favor of mating threats, and again Black cannot take on g5 because of a check on the diagonal a2-g8. This would be a good time for Black to resign.

	25 ...	Qc1 +
	26 Kf2	Qb2 +
	27 Be2	Bf6

The only way to avoid mate, but now Black loses all his material.

	28 Qd5 +	Kg7
	29 Qxb7 +	Kh6
	30 Nf7 +!	Black resigned.

Hopeless, of course, is 30 ... Kg7 31 Nxh8 + or 30 ... Kh5 31 f4 +. The white knight certainly gave a performance on f7 and g5!

(August 1973)

INSPIRATION OR PREPARATION?

**Bronstein vs. Ljubojevic; Alekhine's Defense
Interzonal Tournament, Petropolis 1973**

If I were asked to name the most prolific modern grandmaster in terms of innovative ideas, I would name neither Fischer, Spassky, Larsen, nor Petrosian, but . . . Bronstein!

I speak of new ideas and variations not only on the chessboard but in many other aspects of the game as well. Among Bronstein's myriad suggestions for making chess more lively and interesting are: recording the time used for each move; allowing each player half an hour to finish the game after the first time control; limiting the time for an entire game to one hour; setting up national cup competitions in the form of short matches (the first U.S.S.R. Cup was held in 1970 and was won by Bronstein!); and many others.

His latest suggestion concerns world championship contests. We already have the World Junior Championship, the World Student Team Championship, men's and women's individual titles, men's and women's team titles (the Olympiads) . . . so why not the World Senior Championship? asks Bronstein. His idea is to hold a tournament to which would be invited all grandmasters over the age of fifty who have participated in at least one Candidates' tournament (or match). This proposal has its logic, and perhaps FIDE will deal with it at one of its congresses.

But Bronstein's most interesting and valuable ideas are still produced on the chessboard. I had the pleasure of watching him play at the Interzonal tournament in Petropolis, where among his many magnificent battles his brilliant game against Ljubojevic deserves special mention. Bronstein's rook sacrifice on move sixteen was a tremendous surprise, and during the game it took me quite a while to find the point of it. No wonder this is considered the most beautiful game of the tournament.

At the time I was not sure whether the sacrifice was an improvisation or had been carefully prepared at home. I'm still not sure. Up to move fourteen the players repeated a game between Ljubojevic and Honfi at Cacak 1971. That game was a quick victory for Ljubojevic, who played White. Here against Bronstein he was playing the same variation, but as Black, having in mind an improvement on the fourteenth move. It is that improvement that led to Bronstein's wonderful rook sacrifice two moves later.

Could it have been prepared by Bronstein at home? His sacrifice recalls his famous game with Tal in Riga 1968 [Game 4 in this volume]. He explained his rook sacrifice in that game by saying he "could not miss the opportunity" to play such a move against Tal, an opportunity he might never have again in his whole life. Knowing Bronstein, it's my guess that his sacrifice in this game, too, was an inspiration of the moment—to make the game more interesting, more complicated, more distinct from other games.

In any case, it is a wonderful fighting game and one of the most interesting grandmaster encounters of recent years.

White: David Bronstein
Black: Ljubomir Ljubojevic

Alekhine's Defense

1 e4	Nf6

Ljubojevic usually chooses the Sicilian Defense. His choice of Alekhine's Defense for this game probably means he has prepared an improvement in one of its complicated variations. That would be very hard to meet over the board. But it is not so easy to take Bronstein by surprise in complicated positions!

2 e5	Nd5
3 d4	d6
4 c4	Nb6
5 f4	

The Four Pawns Attack! Is this a smart choice against Ljubojevic, whose main strength lies in complex positions? The move usually seen nowadays is 4 Nf3.

5 ...	dxe5
6 fxe5	c5?!

Ljubojevic probably chose this theoretically inferior continuation to avoid the possibility of a prepared variation in the main line, 6 . . . Bf5. As we will see, however, he is quite at home with the finesses in this variation.

7	d5	e6
8	Nc3	exd5

8 ... Qh4+ 9 g3 Qd4 does not seem entirely logical. Firstly, White can win the exchange with 10 Qe2 exd5 11 Nb5; secondly, Boleslavsky's recommended 10 Bf4! looks even stronger. If Black then takes the pawn with 10 ... g5 11 Bd2 Qxe5+, his position will remain hopelessly exposed after 12 Be2.

9	cxd5	c4

This recommendation by Mikenas is probably Black's best chance. Again the maneuver 9 ... Qh4+ 10 g3 Qd4 looks unnatural and leaves White with a good attacking game after 11 Bb5+ (*11 Bf4 g5 12 Bxg5 Qxe5+ 13 Qe2* is also good for White) 11 ... Bd7 12 Qe2 Nxd5 13 e6! fxe6 14 Qxe6+ Ne7 15 Nf3 (Balashov–Grigorian, Riga 1967).

10	Nf3

This natural developing move looks best, but 10 d6 Nc6 (*11 Nb5!? Qh4+*) and 10 a3 Bc5 must be considered as well.

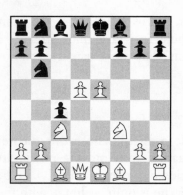

10 ...	Bg4

The other possibility, 10 . . . Bb4, allows 11 Bxc4; e.g., 11 . . . Bxc3 + (according to Boleslavsky, *11 . . . Nxc4 12 Qa4 + Nc6 13 dxc6 Bxc3 + 14 bxc3 b5 15 Qb4! a5 16 Qc5 Qd3 17 Bg5* is good for White) 12 bxc3 Nxc4 13 Qa4 + Nd7 14 Qxc4 Nb6 15 Qb5 + Qd7 (Boleslavsky), and after 16 Qxd7 + and 17 d6 White at least has an extra pawn.

11 Qd4!

Black gets a reasonable position after 11 Bxc4 Nxc4 12 Qa4 + Nd7 13 Qxc4 Bxf3 14 gxf3 Nxe5 (*15 Qe4 Qh4 + !*), although there are still many problems to solve after 15 Qe2!. The text move looks stronger.

11 . . .	Bxf3
12 gxf3	Bb4

12 . . . Nc6 13 Qe4 Nb4 leads to nothing after 14 e6!.

By sacrificing a pawn, Black is able to complete his development and can hope for attacking chances against White's center pawns. The position now becomes very exciting.

13 Bxc4	0-0
14 Rg1	g6!

This is Ljubojevic's prepared improvement. The position was not unfamiliar to him, since two years earlier (Cacak 1971) he had played it with White against Honfi, who chose the weak defense 14 . . . Qc7? and was mated after 15 e6 f6 16 Bh6! Qxc4 17 Rxg7 + Kh8 18 Rg8 + !.

The position now looks critical for White in view of the very unpleasant threat 15 . . . Nc6. After 15 Be3 Black can play 15 . . . N8d7 with the triple threats

16 ... Nxc4, 16 ... Nxe5, and 16 ... Bc5. In this extremely complicated situation, Bronstein finds a wonderful way out.

15 Bg5!   Qc7

White now faces the simultaneous threats of 16 ... Qxc4 and 16 ... Bc5. What can he do?

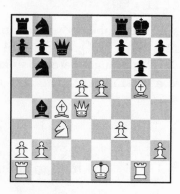

16 Bb3!!

This truly amazing move fully deserves two exclamation marks. White is giving up a whole rook, and at first glance it is not to be seen what he hopes to get for it. The further course of the game, however, will make that clear.

If instead of the text move White tried 16 Be2 Bc5 17 Qf4, the rook could not be taken with 17 ... Bxg1 because of 18 Bf6! with the unavoidable threat of 19 Qh6. But with 17 ... f6! Black could avoid all the mating threats with a good game.

16 ...   Bc5
17 Qf4   Bxg1

The Soviet chess newspaper 64 suggested a line that it claimed refutes the rook sacrifice, but to my mind its conclusions are not convincing.

The first suggestion, 17 ... N8d7 18 d6 Qc6 19 0-0-0 Bxg1 20 Rxg1 Qc5 21 Re1 Rae8, allows the very strong 22 e6!; for instance, 22 ... fxe6 23 Rxe6! Rxf4 24 Rxe8+, or 23 ... Rxe6 24 Bxe6+ Kh8 25 Qxf8+! with mate to follow in either case.

The other suggestion, 17 ... Re8 18 Bf6 N8d7 19 d6 Nxe5 20 Kf1 Bxd6 21 Nb5 Qc6 22 Nxd6 Qxd6 23 Rd1 Qc6 24 Bxe5 Qb5+, is not satisfactory either: after 25 Kg2 Qxe5 26 Qxf7+ Kh8 27 Rge1 Qxb2+ 28 Kh1 White clearly has the better of it. Also, 18 Rg2 Rxe5+ (18 ... Qxe5+? 19 Re2!) 19 Ne4, with many threats, must be considered.

What, in fact, does White have to show for his missing rook? His pieces are excellently developed, his center pawns are very strong, and the enemy king's position is weak and almost undefendable. Still, an entire rook is gone, and what "hard cash" does White have for it?

Direct play for mating threats does not produce results, since 18 Bf6 is adequately met either by 18 ... N8d7 19 Qh6 Nxf6 20 exf6 Qe5+ or by 18 ... Qc5, threatening 19 ... Qe3+. Nor is 18 Ne4 satisfactory, because of 18 ... N8d7. Therefore, White must find a way of combining several methods of attack to exploit Black's backward development and the unfortunate position of the bishop on g1.

First, note that White will get the upper hand if he manages to capture that bishop, since then he will be only an exchange behind. Second, White can allow himself to develop the attack slowly, since Black has no way to achieve active counterplay quickly.

The character of the position makes exhaustive analysis extremely difficult, however, and I hope readers will understand should a hole be found in the following explanations. A position like this is to be played to the end, not analyzed to death!

18 d6

This is a normal move to relieve the pressure against e5 and to open the way for the bishop on b3. Black must now beware of the threat e6, which would be very strong after 18 ... Qc6; for instance, 19 e6! N8d7, and now 20 exf7+ Kg7 21 0-0-0! would lead to a position similar to our later analysis.

Of course, 18 ... Qc5 is bad because White gains valuable tempi with 19 Ne4 Qb4+ 20 Kf1.

18 ...   Qc8

19 Ke2!?

This looks very good, but in fact it exposes White's king too much and gives Black good chances for a successful defense.

In later analysis, both players concluded that 19 0-0-0! is the correct move here. Since 20 Rxg1 is threatened, Black has only two main lines to consider:

A) 19 . . . Bc5 20 e6! N8d7! (the only move; after *20 . . . fxe6* White has *21 Qe5! Re8 22 Be7,* or if *21 . . . Rf7 22 Bxe6 N8d7 23 Bxf7+ Kxf7 24 Qe7+ Kg8 25 Bh6* and Black loses at once) 21 e7, and White regains his material with a decisive attack.

B) 19 . . . Qc5! 20 e6 (*20 Kb1 N8d7* is too slow) 20 . . . N8d7 (Black's best *practical* chance is probably *20 . . . Be3+ 21 Qxe3 Qxe3+ 22 Bxe3 fxe6,* although the ending is clearly in White's favor) 21 exf7+! (*21 e7* wins a rook but gives Black sufficient play after *21 . . . Bxh2!*) 21 . . . Kg7 22 Kb1! and Black, though a rook ahead, seems helpless against the threat of 23 Ne4.

Black can also choose the variation 19 0-0-0 N8d7 20 Rxg1 Qc5, which was mentioned in the analysis after Black's seventeenth move, but it leads to a terrific attack for White after 21 Re1 Rae8 22 e6!.

Another curious idea is 19 Kf1!? (*19 . . . Qc5 20 Ne4*), and if 19 . . . Bc5 then 20 e6 fxe6 (or *20 . . . N8d7 21 exf7+ Kg7 22 Rd1* threatening *23 Ne4*) 21 Qe5 Rxf3+ 22 Ke2. Comprehensive analysis of all these variations would lead us too far afield.

19 . . .   Bc5?

This definitely loses. Black's only reasonable try is 19 . . . Qc5!, giving him excellent chances of repulsing the attack. White then has the following choices:

A) 20 Ne4 Qb5+ 21 Ke1 (or *21 Kd2 Nc4+ 22 Bxc4 Qxb2+!*) 21 . . . N8d7 and Black seems to have adequate defensive resources; for instance, 22 Nf6+ Nxf6 23 Bxf6 Nd7 or 22 Bf6 Nxf6 23 Nxf6+ Kh8.

B) 20 e6 N8d7 (the threat was *21 exf7+* with mate to follow; *20 . . . fxe6 21 Bxe6+* also leads to mate, but worth considering is first *20 . . . Qf2 +* and if *21 Kd1* then *21 . . . Qd4 + 22 Qxd4 Bxd4* is sufficient, or if *21 Kd3* then *21 . . . N8d7* is even stronger, threatening *22 . . . Nc5* mate) *21 exf7 +* (on *21 e7* or *21 exd7*, the answer *21 . . . Qf2 +* and *22 . . . Bxh2* is strong, and *21 Ne4* is met by *21 . . . Qb5 +* and *22 . . . fxe6*, after which there seems to be no promising way for White to continue the attack) *21 . . . Kg7* and Black refutes the attack.

Perhaps I am too pessimistic about White's attacking chances after *19 . . . Qc5!*, but in any case that is clearly the defense Black had to choose. If it were as easy to find the correct defense during the game as it is in later analysis, we certainly wouldn't see many attacking games!

> 20 Ne4   N8d7
> 21 Rc1!

This quiet move is decisive, since Black has no defense against the following sacrifice. A really curious position!

> 21 . . .   Qc6
> 22 Rxc5!

Bronstein still has something to sacrifice! Now Black's king is subjected to a devastating mating attack.

> 22 . . .   Nxc5
> 23 Nf6 +   Kh8

On *23 . . . Kg7*, the reply *24 Qh4!* would be even stronger than it is in the game.

> 24 Qh4!

White doesn't have many pieces left, but the few

that remain create a mating net around Black's king.
There is no longer any reasonable defense.

24 ...   Qb5 +
25 Ke3   h5

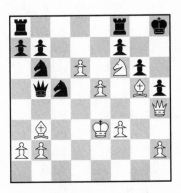

26 Nxh5   Qxb3 +

Desperation, but there is no defense. On 26 ...
Qd3 + 27 Kf2 gxh5 28 Bf6 + mates, and 26 ...
Nd5 + 27 Bxd5 Qd3 + 28 Kf2 Qc2 + 29 Kg3 grants
Black only a brief reprieve. Black can get a little play
with 26 ... Qd3 + 27 Kf2 Ne4 + 28 fxe4 Qd4 +, but
this loses too after 29 Kg2 Qxb2 + 30 Kh3 followed
by 31 Ng3 + and 32 Bf6.

27 axb3   Nd5 +
28 Kd4!

Black was hoping for 28 Kf2 gxh5 29 Qxh5 + Kg8
30 Bf6 Nxf6 31 exf6 Ne6, etc.

28 ...   Ne6 +
29 Kxd5   Nxg5

Now 29 ... gxh5 30 Bf6 + Kg8 31 Ke4 leads to
mate.

| 30 Nf6+ | Kg7 |
| 31 Qxg5 | |

The game is finished. Ljubojevic played on in the hope of taking advantage of his opponent's severe time trouble, but by now things are too easy.

31 ...	Rfd8
32 e6	fxe6+
33 Kxe6	Rf8
34 d7	a5
35 Ng4	Ra6+
36 Ke5	Rf5+
37 Qxf5	gxf5
38 d8Q	fxg4
39 Qd7+	Kh6
40 Qxb7	Rg6
41 f4	Black resigned

A wonderful game!

(December 1973)

SPASSKY'S
BACK IN TOWN

Spassky vs. Rashkovsky, Sicilian Defense
U.S.S.R. Championship, 1973

For some twenty years now, the U.S.S.R. Chess Federation has been wrestling with the problem of how to get its leading players to participate in the national championship. In the 1940s and '50s, as in the years before World War II, this most significant competition was very popular, and almost all the best grandmasters in the country took part in it. But then, probably because of the increasing number of international tournaments, its average strength began to decline, and it has never returned to its former level.

This year the federation tried to restore the championship's strength and importance by introducing a new system. The competition was divided into two tournaments, each with eighteen players. The "top league" included all the players who had qualified for the 1974 candidates' matches and both interzonals, as well as the winners of the four semifinal events that preceded the current championship. This allowed the federation to invite all the leading Soviet grandmasters (with the exception of Botvinnik, who has effectively retired from active tournament play).

The winner would earn the title of U.S.S.R. Champion, the top nine would qualify for next year's "top league," and the next six would qualify for the "first league," a separate event. So aside from the title itself, the most pressing ambition for every player was to finish among the top nine.

The most significant result of this tournament was Boris Spassky's near return to his previous best form. In the many tournaments in which he played after losing the world championship to Bobby Fischer in 1972, Boris seemed unable to pull himself together and did not show us the kinds of games we were accustomed to seeing from him. But in winning this tournament he certainly played the best chess, with interesting opening innovations, complicated middlegame positions, and up-to-date endgame technique.

The following game is a good illustration of his style in this tournament. His handling of a well-known opening poses difficult problems which his opponent is unable to solve.

White: Boris Spassky
Black: N. Rashkovsky

Sicilian Defense

1 e4   c5

For years the most popular response to 1 e4 has been the Sicilian Defense. Today's players prefer these tactical openings, which can be carefully prepared at home, rather than openings in which strategic themes predominate. The same may be said about the King's Indian Defense, one of the most popular answers to 1 d4.

2 Nf3	d6
3 d4	

Among the commonest systems for Black in the Sicilian is the Najdorf Variation, which is what Rashkovsky chooses in this game. An interesting attempt to avoid the Najdorf is 3 Nc3, and if 3 . . . Nf6 White continues 4 e5.

3 . . .	cxd4
4 Nxd4	Nf6
5 Nc3	a6
6 Bg5	

This fashionable move is played by almost everybody, perhaps without even considering other possibilities. We seldom see the old 6 Be2 anymore, and Fischer's favorite 6 Bc4 is only slightly more popular than that. The immediate 6 f4 is practically forgotten, too—but who can say for sure that it's objectively better to develop the bishop to g5 before playing the strategically necessary move f4?

6 . . .	e6
7 f4	Qc7

For a long time, Fischer used to play 7 . . . Qb6 here, accepting the pawn sacrifice 8 Qd2 Qxb2. But the eleventh game of the match with Spassky led him to question the reliability of that system. Theoretically, it may be perfectly all right for Black, but in practice it is always well to remember that White may have exhaustively analyzed the position at home and prepared a new continuation. It is extremely difficult to meet a new attacking system over the board.

The text move, instead of the usual 7 . . . Be7, is a recommendation by Balashov, I believe. In this game the changed order of moves does not lead to new positions, but if Black wants to play this way he must be prepared for the plausible 8 Bxf6 gxf6 9 Be2 followed by Bh5.

8 Bd3!?

White usually uses either of two main systems of development. The most popular is 8 Qf3 followed by 0-0-0. The other is 8 Qe2 and 0-0-0, supporting the strategically important advance e5. Here Spassky introduces what appears to be a new line, first developing the bishop and only then playing his queen to e2. In this game, at least, his idea succeeds.

The question is whether Spassky's idea can be used against the entire system, or only when Black chooses 7 . . . Qc7. After 7 . . . Be7, for instance, 8 Bd3 would be rather dubious because of the possible reply 8 . . . Qb6, or first 8 . . . h6.

8 . . .   Nbd7

By choosing a normal setup for his pieces, Black allows his opponent to carry out his opening plan. It seems to me that 8 . . . Nc6 is the most logical reaction to White's playing his bishop to d3.

```
 9  Qe2       b5
10  0-0-0     Bb7
11  Rhe1!
```

White has completed his development and is already threatening to play e5, which is not easy to meet. Black does not seem to have solved his opening problems satisfactorily.

```
11 ...        Be7
```

This leads to a very strong attacking position for White in which Black will have no practical chances to save the game. But what can be recommended for Black? After 11 ... 0-0-0, the sacrifice 12 Bxb5! is possible. If 11 ... b4, another sacrifice, 12 Nd5! Nxd5 13 exd5 Bxd5 14 Nxe6!, looks very strong. Maybe 11 ... h6 12 Bxf6 gxf6, or 12 Bh4 g5!?, can be tried, but it doesn't look too promising.

```
12  e5!
```

When making this advance White had to calculate accurately the following wild complications, which analysis shows to be clearly in his favor. I don't think Spassky prepared this variation in advance, but decided on it during the game. The fact that he estimated the ensuing complications as favorable for himself over the board is the best proof that he is returning to his previous splendid form.

$$12 \ldots \qquad dxe5$$
$$13 \ fxe5 \qquad Nd5$$

Black probably considered his position acceptable, but it isn't. He saw that White doesn't have time for 14 Nxd5 because of 14 . . . Bxg5 +, and that the exchange 14 Bxe7 allows Black to interpolate 14 . . . Nxc3. But all White's pieces are ready for action, which allows him to add a combinative element that finally decides the game.

14 Bxe7

Probably the strongest line, but 14 Nxe6! Bxg5 + 15 Nxg5 Nxc3 16 bxc3 Qxc3 is also possible. Now 17 Nxf7 allows the defense 17 . . . Qa3 + 18 Kd2 Qa5 + ! 19 c3 Qxa2 + followed by 20 . . . Qxf7. And 17 e6 Qa3 + 18 Kd2 Qb4 + 19 c3 Qb2 + is hardly decisive (*20 Bc2 0-0-0*).

But 17 Qg4! seems to insure a very strong attacking position for White without sacrificing material. On 17 . . . Qa3 + White does not play 18 Kb1 because of 18 . . . Bd5!, but 18 Kd2! (*18 . . . Qa5 + 19 Ke2!*), and Black can't avoid losing material.

White's position is so strong that it's no wonder there's more than one way to get a decisive advantage.

$$14 \ldots \qquad Nxc3$$

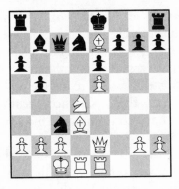

Black has no choice. On 14 . . . Nxe7 the sacrifice
15 Bxb5! is decisive, and after 14 . . . Kxe7 15 Qg4
White simply remains with the much better game.

15 Qg4!

This probably isn't the only way for White to exploit his advantage, but it's undoubtedly the most
elegant and pleasing. Objectively, the simple recapture 15 bxc3 is very strong; for instance: 15 . . . Qxc3
(or *15 . . . Kxe7 16 Qg4*) 16 Qg4! Kxe7 17 Nxe6!
with a decisive attack. If 17 . . . fxe6, then 18 Bxb5!
seems strongest, or if 17 . . . Nxe5 18 Qg5 + f6 19
Qxg7 + Kxe6 20 Bc4 + !, Black will be mated in a few
moves.

15 . . .   Nxd1

Again Black has no choice, since 15 . . . Kxe7 can
be met either by 16 bxc3 or, even better, by 16 Nxe6!
with a winning attack.

16 Nxe6?!

Thus far Spassky has preferred the most beautiful
and surprising lines, and this sacrifice is meant to be

the culmination of the fireworks. A succession of
blows like that is bound to have a demoralizing effect
on the opponent, and experience tells us that under
such conditions a player is unlikely to find the best
replies. Such is the case here, as we will see.

But were all these sacrifices really necessary?
Could White have consummated his advantage more
simply?

On moves 14 and 15, as we have shown, White
could have chosen other ways, though the ones he
chose were just as strong. But this time I think Spassky
goes too far and seriously jeopardizes his advantage.
He should play 16 Bd6!, with the following possibilities:

A) 16 ... Nf2 17 Qxg7 Nxd3 + 18 Kb1 0-0-0 19
cxd3!, and Black will lose his queen.

B) 16 ... Qa5 17 Qg5! f6 (17 ... *Qd8 18 Qxg7*
and *17 ... Nf6 18 Rxd1* are not worth discussing) 18
Qh5 + Kd8 19 Nxe6 + Kc8 20 Rxd1 with a decisive
advantage.

C) 16 ... Qb6 17 Qg5 Nf6 18 exf6 Qxd6 (or *18
... 0-0-0 19 Rxe6 Rhg8 20 Bc5*) 19 Nf5! or fxg7
with a winning attack.

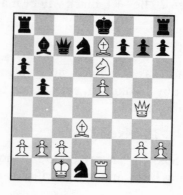

16 . . .   Qc6?

It's easy to lose your way after receiving so many unpleasant surprises from your opponent. No wonder Black misses his best defense, 16 . . . fxe6!.

Even then, White still has a strong attack, of course, but I could not find a clear line that gives him a definite advantage, let alone a win. Maybe I did not analyze deeply enough and there is in fact a win for White after 16 . . . fxe6!, but there can be no doubt that this is the defense Black should have chosen.

Here are some of the variations I examined and the conclusions I arrived at after long study of the possibilities after 16 . . . fxe6. The critical position is reached after 17 Bd6 (not *17 Qxe6 Nf8!*) 17 . . . Qb6! (much better than *17 . . . Qa5 18 Qxe6+ Kd8 19 Bf5 Bc6 20 Be7+ Kc7 21 Rxd1*) 18 Qxe6+ Kd8.

Position after 18 . . . Kd8 (analysis)

Here I looked at the following lines:

A) 19 Qe7+ Kc8 20 e6 (on *20 Bf5* Black can play *20 . . . Qd8*, as he can also after *20 Rxd1*) 20 . . . Nf6 21 Qxg7 Re8 and Black is safe.

B) 19 Rxd1 Re8 20 Qf7 Qe3+ 21 Kb1 Bc6, and thanks to the threat of . . . Rxe5, Black is safe here, too (*22 Bf5 Qe2!*).

C) 19 Bf5 Bc6 20 Qe7+ (*20 Rxd1 Re8 21 Qf7 Qe3+ 22 Kb1 Qe2!* leads to variation B above; or if *20 Be7+ Kc8 21 Rxd1*, Black has the good defense *21 . . . Ra7!*; the quiet *20 Qf7*, threatening *21 e6* gives Black time to consolidate his position with *20 . . . Ne3 21 Ba3 Qd4*, etc.) 20 . . . Kc8 21 e6 (on *21 Rxd1* the counterattack *21 . . . Qe3+ 22 Kb1 Qe2* is annoying) 21 . . . Nf6 (*21 . . . Nb8* can be considered, too) 22 Qxg7 Re8 23 Rxd1 (or *23 Qxf6 Ne3* and White has four pawns against a rook) 23 . . . Qe3+ (after *23 . . . Ng8 24 b4* White can create some annoying threats) 24 Kb1 Nd5!, and again White has to prove that his pawns and positional pressure are sufficient compensation for his missing rook.

The situation is extremely complicated, and it is possible that White's attack can be strengthened at some point. This position is a good project for analysts who like complications!

17 Nxg7+   Kxe7
18 Qg5+

Less convincing is 18 e6 Nf6 19 Nf5+ Kd8.

18 . . .   f6

After 18 . . . Kf8 19 Nf5! Black has no adequate defense against the threats 20 Qg7+, 20 Qe7+, and 20 e6; e.g., 19 . . . Qxg2 20 Qe7+ Kg8 21 e6!, or 19 . . . Qg6 20 Qe7+ Kg8 21 e6, in either case with a decisive attack.

19 exf6+   Kd8
20 f7+   Kc7

Or 20 . . . Qf6 (*20 . . . Nf6 21 Re6*) 21 Re8 + Kc7 22 Qg3 + and now 22 . . . Qd6 (*22 . . . Kb6 23 Re6 +*) 23 Ne6 + wins the queen.

21 Qf4 +   Black resigned

On 21 . . . Kb6 22 Re6, White wins the queen and keeps his attack, or if 21 . . . Qd6 22 Ne6 + leads to the same result.

The audience greeted Spassky's fine victory with prolonged applause.

(January 1974)

WHO STOOD BETTER? WHO KNOWS?

**Tal vs. Petrosian; Caro-Kann Defense
U.S.S.R. Championship, Moscow 1973**

It would be hard to find two leading grandmasters whose playing styles are as dissimilar as those of Tal and Petrosian. These two former world champions approach the game from diametrically opposite positions. Tal likes to attack; Petrosian prefers to defend. Tal enjoys complications, combinations, and sacrifices; Petrosian feels most comfortable in relatively quiet positions, especially where the strategies are clear and there is little danger for himself. Tal is always ready to take any kind of risk; for Petrosian the first order of business is the security of his own position.

A game between these two grandmasters is always an event of great interest. Not for them a dull game of endless maneuvering with an inconclusive outcome. On the contrary, we expect an uncompromising fight in which both players use their resources to the utmost—Tal attacking fiercely, Petrosian defending coolly—and in which it is impossible to say whether the attack or the defense will prevail.

Most games between them are in fact like that, but not all. We have seen magnificent attacks by Petrosian and wonderful defensive achievements by Tal. Grandmasters of this class know their job in all kinds of positions, though they prefer, of course, those that suit their personal styles.

This clash of styles lent special interest to their game in the 1973 Soviet Championship. After achieving a slight initiative against Petrosian's Caro-Kann Defense, Tal chose a rather risky (but not for Tal!) line in which the two sides castled on opposite wings. Here there was no question of attack versus defense: both sides clearly had to attack. But could Petrosian be a match for Tal when it came to direct attack against the king?

This time he was. Black's attack was slightly more advanced and his threats the more dangerous ones, so Tal had to do something to protect his king. But he didn't find the right way, almost got into a mating net, and lost material—which of course meant loss of the game.

Tal's twentieth move appears to have been a mistake, but who would dare say positively what the outcome would have been with best play on both sides? The position on the board was so complicated that the two players themselves, in their post-game analysis, could not agree on who stood better.

After the most prolonged analysis of the critical position, I myself still hesitate to give a definite opinion. It is all too easy to overlook something, even in home analysis, when there are so many complicated possibilities. I would not be surprised to learn that some of my conclusions are not perfectly accurate, or that there's an error somewhere in all that complicated analysis.

I've used my knowledge and experience to try to explain what was happening in this most interesting game. To those chess fans who would rather not spend the time and energy analyzing it for themselves, I wish many happy hours of real chess entertainment.

White: Mikhail Tal
Black: Tigran Petrosian

Caro-Kann Defense

1 e4   c6

Tal's opponents usually try to find convenient ways to avoid giving him positions that lead to complications or attacking possibilities. The Caro-Kann, an opening in which quiet positional play generally predominates, is a sensible choice against Tal.

2 d4	d5
3 Nc3	dxe4
4 Nxe4	Nd7

The main line, 4 ... Bf5, gives White a lasting initiative and prospects of an endgame advantage. The more ambitious text move usually leads to an exciting middlegame in which White gets some initiative but Black has a solid position with reasonable counterplay.

| 5 Bc4 | Ngf6 |
| 6 Ng5 | |

White can get a relatively quiet game and some initiative with 6 Nxf6+ Nxf6. But this does not suit Tal's style and he chooses a more complicated line, probably the most unpleasant one for Black in this variation.

$$6 \ldots \qquad e6$$
$$7 \ Qe2 \qquad Nb6$$

Black is hardly likely to overlook the obvious threat 8 Nxf7.

$$8 \ Bb3$$

This position is well known to opening theorists, who claim adequate counterplay for Black after 8 Bd3 h6 9 N5f3 c5.

$$8 \ldots \qquad a5$$

The strategic necessity for Black in positions like this is . . . c5, beginning a counteraction in the center. That advance can be combined with moves like . . . h6 and . . . a5, which can be played in any order. Though the usual continuation is 8 . . . h6 (*9 Ne4? Qxd4!*), the text move is also good.

Perhaps a little less exact is 8 . . . c5 9 N1f3, since 9 . . . cxd4 10 0-0 and 11 Rd1 gives White his pawn back with an excellent game. In this line, 9 . . . h6 can be met by 10 Ne4.

A bad mistake is 8 . . . Qxd4 9 N1f3, and Black loses his f-pawn after 10 Ne5 (*9 . . . Bb4+? 10 c3 Bxc3+ 11 Kf1!*).

$$9 \ a4$$

This is a new move, but it's hardly preferable to the old 9 a3. The trap 9 . . . Qxd4? 10 N1f3 Bb4+ 11 c3

Bxc3 + 12 Kf1 Qb4 13 Qd1! is not sufficient justification for White's experiment, and if White castles queenside the advanced a-pawn can become a serious weakness.

      9 . . .   h6
      10 N5f3   c5

Having accomplished this necessary advance, Black begins his usual counteraction in the center, which generally enables him to achieve a satisfactory game. White's most reasonable line now is 11 dxc5 Bxc5 12 Ne5 followed by 13 Ngf3 and 0-0. But Tal has some rather "crazy" ideas in mind.

      11 Bf4   Bd6

Petrosian is not a player who likes unclear sacrifices, but if Tal were playing Black he might consider 11 . . . Nfd5 12 Be5 c4!? 13 Bxc4 Bb4 + 14 Kf1 (*14 c3 Nxc3!*) 14 . . . Nxc4 15 Qxc4 b6, with active play for the pawn.

      12 Be5   0-0
      13 0-0-0?!

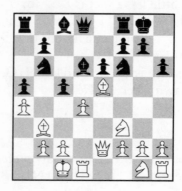

"Tal must be crazy!" That was the first reaction by his grandmaster colleagues and by the public. And with good reason: castling on the queenside after playing a4 really looks suicidal. Objectively, the move cannot be approved.

But there's another side to the coin, which makes Tal's decision understandable. This game was played at the end of the tournament, when Tal desperately needed points. The text move creates a situation in which quiet play is out of the question and all-out attack by both sides is required. Since this kind of situation is ideal for Tal and most uncomfortable for Petrosian, Tal may have been hoping he could outplay his opponent. But in order to get the kind of position he wants, Tal is giving his rival considerable odds, since in the following race it is Black who comes first.

A solid continuation is 13 dxc5 Bxc5 14 Nh3 followed by 15 0-0. Or 13 Rd1 leads to a middlegame rich in possibilities.

13 . . .   c4!

A very strong reply, eliminating the white a-pawn and thus opening the way for Black's own a-pawn. Black is already starting operations against the white king while White has yet to complete his development on the kingside.

14 Bxc4   Nxa4
15 Nh3   Nb6
16 g4

White starts his action, but Black's is already under way. The complications quickly reach a climax as White's g-pawn and Black's a-pawn tear up the enemy positions. In the race to be first, Black is an important tempo ahead.

16 ...   a4!

Black can try to meet the threat 17 g5 in other ways; e.g., 16 ... Nxc4 17 Qxc4 b5 has its positive points. Instead, he opts for a race between attacking pawns, hoping to exploit the fact that he is a tempo ahead. This seems to be the correct decision, as the game shows.

17 g5   hxg5
18 Nhxg5

It's hard to tell whether 18 Nfxg5 would have been better, but after 18 ... a3 19 b3 Bb4 or 19 ... Nbd5 I see no reason to think so. The opening of the d1-h5 diagonal for the queen is meaningless, and the knight looks no better on h3 than on f3.

All White has to do now is put a rook on the g-file to get a terrific attacking position. But it's Black's move!

18 ...   a3!

A terribly uncomfortable move for White. The main threat is 19 ... axb3+ followed by 20 ... Na4+ or 20 ... Ba3+, which is very hard to meet. So Tal decides to leave the enemy pawn on a3, but it creates most unpleasant threats against the king. The fight is nearing its climax.

19 b3   Bb4!?

Petrosian misses the better line 19 ... Nbd5!, which not only threatens 20 ... Nc3 or 20 ... Bb4 but also opens the important d8-a5 diagonal for the black queen. Here are some interesting possibilities:

Position after 19 ... Nbd5 (analysis)

A) 20 Bxd5 a2! 21 Kb2 Ba3+ 22 Ka1 Qa5 23 Qd3 (*23 Rd3 Bb2+!*) 23 ... Bb4! 24 Kb2 exd5 25 Bxf6 Bf5! 26 Qe3 Rfc8 and Black wins (*27 c4 a1Q+! 28 Rxa1 Ba3+ 29 Rxa3 Qxa3+ 30 Kc3 Rxc4+*).

B) 20 Rdg1 a2 21 Kb2 Qa5! (or *21 ... Bb4 22 Ne4!*) 22 Ne4 (also hopeless is *22 Qd3 a1Q+! 23 Rxa1 Ba3+ 24 Kb1 Nc3+*) 22 ... a1Q+ (possible is *22 ... Bxe5 23 Nxe5 Nxe4!*) 23 Rxa1 Ba3+ 24 Kb1 Nxe4 and wins.

C) 20 Rhg1!? gives Black two ways to pursue his attack. After 20 ... a2 21 Kb2 Qa5 the continuation 22 Ne4 loses because of 22 ... Bxe5 23 Nxe5 (*23 dxe5 Nxe4* or *23 Bxd5 exd5* doesn't help) 23 ... Nxe4!, and now the sacrifice 24 Rxg7+ Kxg7 25 Qg4+ Kf6 26 Qh4+ Ng5 27 Qh6+ Ke7 28 Qxg5+ Kd6 is not good enough for White. However, the surprising line 22 Qd3 a1Q+ (*22 ... Bb4 23 Ne4!*) 23 Rxa1 Ba3+ 24 Kb1 Nc3+ (*24 ... Qc3 25 Rxa3*) 25 Qxc3 Qxc3 26 d5! offers White some attacking chances to compensate for his queen.

Therefore, on 20 Rhg1 the answer 20 ... Nc3! seems much simpler, with the following possibilities: 21 Qd3 a2 22 Kd2 (or *22 Kb2 Nxd1+ 23 Rxd1*

Bxe5, etc.) 22 ... Nxd1! (the simplest) 23 Bxf6 Qa5+ 24 Ke2! (*24 Kxd1 Qf5!*) 24 ... Nc3+ 25 Ke3 Qf5 26 Qxf5 exf5 27 Nxf7 Rxf7! 28 Rxg7+ Kf8 29 Rxf7+ Ke8 and White's attack is exhausted.

D) 20 Qd3! is undoubtedly White's best answer to 19 ... Nbd5 and offers him good chances to hold the position. The point is that after 20 ... a2 21 Kb2 Black cannot play 21 ... Qa5 because his bishop is hanging, and on 21 ... Bb4 White gets out of trouble with 22 Bxf6! Nxf6 23 c3. The attack 21 ... Ba3+ 22 Ka1 Qa5 (*22 ... Bb4 23 Bxf6!*) is also not fully convincing after 23 Rhg1 (*23 ... Bb4 24 Ne4!*).

Black's best chance after 20 Qd3 seems to be 20 ... Nb4!, forcing the reply 21 Qd2, and now he may proceed 21 ... b5! (also *21 ... Nfd5* is worth considering) 22 Bxb5 Nfd5 or 22 ... Ba6 (or *22 ... Bb7*), with excellent attacking chances. Further analysis of this position would take us too far afield, but Black seems to have the upper hand.

20 Rdg1?

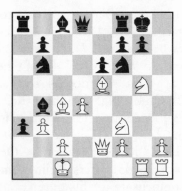

This loses immediately. It is interesting that Tal, even in a position where he should be giving first consideration to the safety of his king, thinks only of attacking possibilities. The white king is in far more danger than its adversary, and steps have to be taken now to protect it.

Other methods of direct attack are also inadequate; e.g., 20 Rhg1 a2 (*20 . . . Bc3* is also good) 21 Kb2 Nfd5! with a decisive attack (*22 Ne4 f6,* or *22 Bxd5 Nxd5 23 Rd3 f6 24 Qe4 fxg5 25 Nxg5 Qxg5!*); or 20 Qd3 a2 21 Kb2 Nxc4+ 22 bxc4 (*22 Qxc4 Nd5!*) 22 . . . Qb6 23 Qb3 Ra3 and wins.

With the text move Tal has in mind the crazy variation 20 . . . Bc3 21 Qd3! a2 22 Kd1 a1Q+ 23 Ke2 with wild complications. But here too Black has an adequate defense with 23 . . . Nbd5!; for instance, 24 Bxd5 exd5 25 Bxf6 Qe8+ followed by 26 . . . Qa6, or 24 Nh7 Nf4+ 25 Bxf4 Nxh7 and the attack is refuted.

Tal would not be so badly off if he had first given his king a flight square with 20 c3!. After 20 . . . Bxc3 (*20 . . . a2 21 Kc2*) 21 Qd3!, the two threats 22 Bxf6 and 22 Qxc3 practically force the moves 21 . . . Bb2+ 22 Kb1. But now that his king is no longer in a mating net, White has time to revive his attack. The killing threat is 23 Bxf6; e.g., 22 . . . Nxc4 23 Bxf6 a2+ 24 Kc2.

I see nothing better for Black (after *20 c3 Bxc3 21 Qd3 Bb2+ 22 Kb1*) than 22 . . . g6, since 22 . . . Nbd7 23 Rhg1 Nxe5 24 Nxe5 would leave White with a fine game.

White has a good choice of attacking lines here, of which the following are worth mentioning:

A) 23 Nxe6?! Qe7!? (*23 . . . Bxe6 24 Bxe6 Kg7 25 Rhg1* gives White a decisive attack, as does *23 . . . Qe8 24 Nc7! Bf5 25 Qxf5 gxf5 26 Nxe8*, and on *23*

Position after 22 . . . g6 (analysis)

. . . a2 + White has the simple answer *24 Kc2!*) 24
Rhg1! (*24 Nxf8? Bf5!*) 24 . . . Nxc4 (*24 . . . Bxe6 25
Bxe6 fxe6 26 Qxg6+ Kh8 27 Rg3! Qh7 28 Rh3!*, or
*25 . . . Qxe6 26 Rxg6+ fxg6 27 Qxg6+ Kh8 28
Qh6+ Kg8 29 Rg1+ Kf7 30 Ng5+ Ke7 31 Nxe6
Kxe6 32 Bxf6 Rxf6 33 Re1+ and wins*) 25 Rxg6+
fxg6 26 Qxg6+ Kh8 27 Nxf8 (*27 Qh6+ Qh7+!*, or
27 Rg1 Nxe5) 27 . . . Nxe5 28 Nxe5 (*28 dxe5 Qxe6*)
28 . . . Qg7! and Black holds.

But in answer to 23 Nxe6 Black can choose the
more interesting reply 23 . . . Nxc4!. This looks bad
at first because of 24 Nxd8 Nxe5 25 Nxe5! Bf5 26
Qxf5! gxf5 27 Rhg1+ with strong pressure (*27 . . .
Kh7 28 Rd3*). But after 24 Nxd8 the real point is 24
. . . Nd5!!. In this amazing position Black is threatening mate in two beginning with 25 . . . a2+, so
White is practically forced to take the knight. On 25
Qxc4 Bf5+ 26 Ka2 Rfxd8 White is in trouble (*27
Rc1 Bd3!*), and 25 bxc4 allows the following fantas-
tic finish: 25 . . . Nb4! 26 Ne1 (*26 Qe4 Bc3 and 27
. . . a2+*) 26 . . . Bf5! 27 Qxf5 Bc3!! 28 Nc2 (*28 Qc2
a2+, or 28 Rd2 Bxd2 29 d5 gxf5*) 28 . . . a2+ 29

Kc1 Rfxd8! 30 Na1 gxf5 and wins. A truly incredible variation!

B) 23 Bxe6 Bxe6 24 Nxe6 Qe8! (bad is *24 . . . Qc8 25 Rhg1! Qxe6 26 Rxg6+*, etc., and White gets a reasonable game after *24 . . . Qe7 25 Nxf8* [*25 Rhg1 Nbd5!*] *25 . . . Kxf8 26 Ng5* or *26 Rdg1*) 25 Nc7 (*25 Nxf8 Nfd5* gives Black strong counterplay, but *25 Rhg1* is to be considered) 25 . . . Qc6 26 Nxa8 (*26 d5? Nbxd5 27 Nxd5 Nxd5 28 Qxd5? a2+ 29 Kxb2 a1Q+!*) 26 . . . Rxa8 and Black has full compensation for the exchange.

C) 23 Rhg1 Nxc4! 24 bxc4 (*24 Nxe6* is refuted by *24 . . . Nxe5! 25 Nxe5 Bxe6 26 Rxg6+ fxg6 27 Qxg6+ Kh8*; the alternative *24 Nxf7 Kxf7 25 Qxg6+ Ke7* is not clear; and after *24 Qxc4* the reply *24 . . . Nd5* seems to hold everything) 24 . . . Qb6! 25 Ka2 Bc1! (the saving move!) 26 Qb3 (*26 d5 Qb2+! 27 Bxb2 axb2+ 28 Kb3 Ra3+! 29 Kxa3 b1Q+ 30 Rxc1 Qxd3+*, or *29 Kc2 Rxd3 30 Rxd3 exd5* wins for Black) 26 . . . Qxb3+ 27 Kxb3 Bxg5 28 Nxg5 Ne8, and the endgame should offer both sides roughly equal chances.

As we have seen, the position is enormously complicated and the fate of the game often hangs by a single slim thread. Perhaps White can get something more out of the position—for instance, 23 Nd2 opens the way for the queen to get to h3—but we will leave the analysis of this and other possibilities to the reader.

One thing is clear: White had to play 20 c3!, which would have led to fascinating complications with a quite unpredictable outcome.

20 . . .   a2!

Tal must have underestimated the strength of this advance.

                21 Kb2   Nxc4+

Even simpler than 21 ... Nfd5 22 Bxd5 Nxd5 23 Ne4 f6 with the same effect.

                22 Qxc4

Or 22 bxc4 Qb6 and wins (*23 c5 Be1+!*).

                22 ...   Nd5!

With a few strong moves Petrosian has completely repulsed White's attack and now has an easily won position.

                23 Ne4

The attack 23 Nxe6 is refuted by 23 ... a1Q+!, and after 23 Bxg7 the simplification 23 ... Bc3+ 24 Qxc3 Nxc3 25 Nxe6 a1Q+! is good enough.

Now the game is over. What a pity that Tal missed the right line, 20 c3!.

                23 ...   f6
                24 Bf4

There is nothing to be done; 24 Bg3 f5 is equally hopeless.

24 . . .	Ba3 +
25 Ka1	Nxf4

An extra piece and the better position—that's too big an advantage to give Petrosian!

26 h4	Rf7
27 Rg4	Qa5
White resigned	

Both players may be proud of this tremendous battle, with its many beautiful points and wonderful variations, and I'm sure all real chess enthusiasts will enjoy it very much. I beg the reader's indulgence for any flaws that may be found in the analysis of all those intricate complications—this was too much even for home analysis!

(April 1974)

A TALE OF
TWO KNIGHTS

**Keres vs. Taimanov; Queen's Indian Defense
Tallinn 1975**

The Tallinn International Tournament, which has been organized every two years since 1969, has become a pleasant tradition. This time, despite various difficulties—which all organizers of international tournaments face these days—we were able to put together a representative and rather strong competition. With nine grandmasters among the sixteen participants, it was in fact one of the strongest of the year.

We were disappointed, however, at the last-minute withdrawals of some top grandmasters. Among those we missed were former world champion Tal, Korchnoi (who was playing his Candidates' Final match with Karpov), Robert Byrne and Polugaevsky (both of whom were occupied with other business), and Unzicker.

But a number of interesting personalities did attend, and they helped create a very friendly atmosphere. Although there were problems, I think I may say that our guests enjoyed both the tournament and their stay in our old city, and I hope we will have the pleasure of welcoming them again next time.

As it happened, I finished clear first. Olafsson and Spassky tied for second and third, and Bronstein and Hort tied for fourth and fifth. Due to the rather unsatisfactory state of my health I was considering retiring from active play in the near future. But now I'm not so sure!

Of the many good games played in this tournament, I offer my encounter with Grandmaster Taimanov. Played in the twelfth round, it was very important in determining the final placement of the winners.

White: Paul Keres
Black: Mark Taimanov

Queen's Indian Defense

1 d4	Nf6
2 Nf3	e6

This surprised me. Taimanov usually prefers some form of Indian setup with 2 . . . g6.

3 c4	b6
4 e3	

The system with 4 g3 is more popular, but I think the text leads to a more complicated middlegame.

4 . . .	Bb7
5 Bd3	Be7

                    6 0-0   0-0
                    7 b3   c5
                    8 Bb2

The idea of saddling Black with hanging pawns
with 8 dxc5 bxc5 9 Bb2 d5 10 cxd5 exd5 can be
avoided with 9 . . . d6, leaving open the possibility of
. . . e5.

                    8 . . .   cxd4
                    9 exd4   d5
                   10 Nbd2

Through a different order of moves, the position
after 10 Nc3 dxc4 11 bxc4 Nc6 12 Qe2 arose in a
game between the same opponents in the 1951
U.S.S.R. Championship. Taimanov could have cre-
ated great complications with 12 . . . Nb4, with the
possibility 13 Bb1 Bxf3 14 Qxf3 Qxd4. Considering
my good standing in the tournament, I saw no reason
to plunge into such unclear complications.

                   10 . . .   Nc6
                   11 Rc1   Rc8
                   12 Qe2

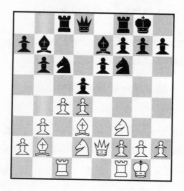

This is a typical position in this variation. White has some advantage in space and chances to be active in the center and on the kingside. His main goal is to accomplish the maneuver Ne5 under favorable conditions, while Black must take measures against this positional threat. White can also think about starting action on the queenside with . . . c5.

Though Black is in no immediate danger, he does have a problem: no active counterplay. His following maneuver is aimed at supporting the eventual center push . . . e5 and blocking the critical diagonal of White's bishop on d3, once White has played c5. This is considered Black's most sensible plan in this position.

12 . . .	Re8
13 Rfd1	Bf8
14 Qe3	

This prepares Ne5, which would be premature now because of 14 . . . dxc4, attacking the d-pawn in a most uncomfortable way.

| 14 . . . | g6 |
| 15 h3 | |

But again not 15 Ne5 because of 15 . . . dxc4, and if 16 bxc4 Nxe5 17 dxe5 Bc5 followed by 18 . . . Ng4, and White has problems, or if 16 Nxc6 Rxc6 17 bxc4, then 17 . . . Bg7 with a reasonable game for Black.

| 15 . . . | Nh5 |

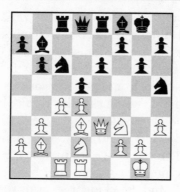

Black has done everything he could and must now decide on his further plans. The text move prepares to meet 16 Ne5 with 16 ... dxc4 17 bxc4?! Nxe5 18 dxe5 Bc5. But the knight is badly placed on h5, and it remains a problem for him till the end of the game. I would have preferred 15 ... Bg7, waiting for White to reveal his plans.

16 Nf1

Also worth considering is 16 g4 Nf6 17 Ne5, further restricting Black's freedom of movement. But with a pleasant position like this, you want to leave it as it is and enjoy it for a while.

White now intends N1h2-g4, with an eye toward exploiting the weaknesses on his opponent's kingside.

16 ...   Qd6
17 N1h2

But not 17 c5 bxc5 18 dxc5 Qf4, and Black's majority in the center is worth more than White's on the queenside. After the text move, neither 17 ... Qf4 18 Qe2 nor 17 ... Nf4 18 Bf1 improves Black's position.

17 . . .	Bg7
18 Ne5	

By occupying this strategically important point, White further reduces Black's mobility and virtually forces him to trade pieces on that square (if *18 . . . Red8 19 Nhg4*, threatening *20 Nh6+*). But Black will then still have to deal with the problem of his misplaced knight, not to mention the weakness of the dark squares on his kingside.

18 . . .	dxc4
19 bxc4	Nxe5
20 dxe5	Qc5
21 Bd4	Qc6
22 Bf1	

The exchanges have given Black some space for his pieces and some counterplay on the a8-h1 diagonal. But his main problems—that misplaced knight and those kingside weaknesses—remain.

22 . . .	Red8
23 Ng4	Rd7
24 Rd2	Rcd8
25 Rcd1	Qe4

Black's activity during his last few moves was only temporary and brought him no essential relief.

To keep his attacking possibilities, White must avoid exchanging queens.

26 Qc3!	Qc6

Slightly better is 26 . . . Nf4 27 f3 Qc6 (if *28 Be3? Nd5!*), creating a weakness for White at g3 and closing the d1-h5 diagonal for his bishop. But 28 Qe3

Nh5 29 Kh2 retains all the advantages of the White position.

After the game, Taimanov told me that he considered his position entirely satisfactory at this point. His last move was a tacit draw offer (27 Qe3 Qe4), but White has other plans.

27	Be3	Bf8
28	Bg5	Rxd2
29	Rxd2	Rd7
30	Nh6 +	Kg7

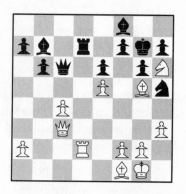

The point of the knight check was to see whether Black was afraid of 31 Bf6 + Nxf6 32 exf6 +, after which he could play 32 ... Kh8! (but not *32 ... Kxh6? 33 Qe3 + g5 34 h4!*). Black has to avoid answering 30 Nh6 + with 30 ... Kh8 because of 31 Rd6!.

31 Ng4

Interesting complications might have followed 31 Qf3 Qxf3 32 Rxd7!, but Black has the good and simple defense 31 ... Qc7!. Or if 31 Rxd7 Qxd7 32 g4, Black has the reply 32 ... Be7!; e.g. 33 Bxe7 Qxe7, or 33 Bc1 Qc6 34 f3 Ng3, etc.

But 31 Rxd7 Qxd7 32 Be2!, threatening 33 Bxh5
gxh5 34 Bf6 + !, looks very strong. On 32 ... Be7
White plays 33 Bc1, maintaining the threat 34 Bxh5;
e.g., 33 ... Be4 34 g4!, or 33 ... Kf8 34 Bxh5 gxh5
35 Qg3 Qd1 + 36 Kh2 Ke8 37 Bg5! with various
threats.

With time pressure approaching, however, exact
calculation of all the possibilities was impossible.

31 ...	Kg8
32 Rd3	Rxd3

White would have forced this exchange anyway,
with 33 Qd2.

33 Qxd3	Qc7
34 Be2	Be7

It's hard for Black to find a reasonable move. This
one will at least give some protection to the dark
squares on the kingside or eliminate White's strong
bishop. On 35 Bc1 he has the good defense 35 ...
Qd8.

35 Bxe7	Qxe7
36 Qd6!	Qf8

This leads to loss of material, but trading queens
with 36 ... Qxd6 37 exd6 leads to a practically hopeless endgame after 37 ... Kf8 38 Bd1! (threatening
39 Ba4 and 40 Ne5). The main source of Black's
troubles is still his knight on h5.

37 Qc7	Be4

37 ... Qc8 38 Qe7, etc., is no better.

38 Qxa7	Qa8

On 38 ... Qb4 the answer 39 Nf6 + ! is very

strong, or on 38 . . . Kg7 White simply takes another
pawn: 39 Qxb6.

39 Qe7

In time trouble, and with such a simple win as 39
Qxa8 + Bxa8 40 Nf6 + !, why look for complications?

39 . . .   Kg7

After 39 . . . Qxa2 40 Nh6 + Kg7 41 Qxf7 + Kxh6
42 Qf8 + Black gets mated; e.g., 42 . . . Ng7 43 Qf4 +
g5 44 Qf6 + Bg6 45 f4!, or 42 . . . Kg5 43 f4 + ! Nxf4
(*43 . . . Kh4 44 Qd8 +*) 44 h4 +, etc.

Also not good is 39 . . . Bb7 40 Nh6 + Kg7 41
Nxf7.

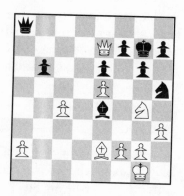

40 Qg5?

White again misses the clear path: 40 Nf6! Nxf6
41 exf6 + Kg8 42 Bg4. With the text, the last move
before the time control, he seriously jeopardizes his
win.

Things are a bit more complicated after 40 . . .
Nf4, but even then 41 Bf1 makes things fairly easy for

White; for instance, 41 ... Bxg2 42 Ne8 + Kg8 43
Nc7! Qe4 (or *43 ... Qc6 44 Qd8 + Kg7 45 Ne8 +
and White wins after either 45 ... Kh6 46 Qh4 +
Nh5 47 Bf3 or 45 ... Kg8 46 Nd6 + Kg7 47 Qf6 +*)
44 Qd8 + Kg7 45 Ne8 + Kh6 46 Qh4 + Nh5 47 f4!
and Black loses a piece.

40 ...   Qxa2!

The time pressure is over, along with most of
White's advantage. Material equality has been re-
stored, and the attack 41 Qh6 + Kg8 42 Nf6 + Nxf6
43 exf6 is refuted by 43 ... Qa1 + and 44 ... Qxf6.
White will have to work hard to win this game all
over again. As before, his main chance is Black's bad
knight and the weak squares surrounding Black's
king.

41 Kh2!?   Qb2?

On 41 ... Qxe2 the above line works: 42 Qh6 +,
etc. Black's only try is 41 ... Kf8!, threatening to take
the bishop. Then 42 Qh6 + followed by 43 Qe3
would leave White with some advantage, but the final
outcome would still be in some doubt.

Instead of 41 Kh2, therefore, White should have
first played 41 Qh6 + and only after 41 ... Kg8 continued 42 Kh2!.

42 Qh6 +   Kg8
43 Qe3   Bb1

This unnatural move is practically forced, since the
bishop can't leave the b1-h7 diagonal because of 44
Nh6 + followed by 45 Bxh5. On 43 ... Qc2 the
maneuver 44 Nf6 + Nxf6 45 exf6 is decisive.

The game was adjourned here and White sealed his
next move.

44 Nh6 +   Kf8

If 44 ... Kg7 45 g4 Nf4 46 Qxf4 Qxe2 47 Qxf7 +
Kxh6 48 Qf8 + Kg5 49 Kg3! with mate to follow.

45 g4

Also possible, and probably simpler, is 45 c5! bxc5
46 g4, winning a piece (46 ... Ng7 47 Qxc5 +). The
endgame after 46 ... Qd4 47 Qxd4 cxd4 48 gxh5 d3
49 Bf3 gxh5 50 Bxh5 Bc2 (50 ... d2 51 Bd1!) 51
Ng4 Bd1 52 Kg3 d2 53 Kh4! followed by 54 Ne3 is
an easy win for White.

45 ...   Ng7

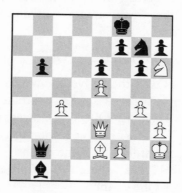

46 c5!

White has to handle the position very carefully.
Though 46 Qf4 looks very strong, the ending after
the surprise piece sacrifice 46 ... Bf5! 47 gxf5 (or 47
Bf1 g4!) 47 ... exf5 followed by 48 ... Ne6 would
be difficult, if not impossible, for White to win because of the miserable position of his knight—a curious echo of Black's knight problem throughout the
game.

White's last move leads to the creation of a passed pawn, since 46 . . . bxc5 loses immediately to 47 Qxc5 + .

46 . . .   b5
47 c6   Ne8
48 Qf4!

Only now is this move decisive. After 48 . . . f5 49 exf6, Black can't recapture because then White's c-pawn promotes. Black must therefore give up a piece, but this time under more unfavorable conditions than in the previous note.

48 . . .   Bf5
49 gxf5   exf5
50 Qe3!

In spite of his extra piece, it is not easy for White to realize his advantage. Trying to force matters with 50 e6 fxe6 51 c7 Qc3 (better than *51 . . . Qc2 52 Qb4 +! Kg7 53 Qe7 +! Kxh6 54 Qf8 +! Kg5 55 h4 + Kf4 56 Qb4 +*, and then *56 . . . Ke5 57 c8Q! Qxc8 58 f4 +* leads to mate) 52 Bc4 unnecessarily gives Black counterchances with 52 . . . e5!.

50 . . .   Nc7

On 50 . . . Kg7 White wins with 51 e6! fxe6 52 Qxe6 Nc7 53 Nxf5 + gxf5 54 Qe7 + Kg6 55 Qd6 +!, etc.

51 Bf3   b4

Nothing is changed by 51 . . . Kg7 52 Kg2 threatening 53 Nxf5 +, and on 51 . . . Ne6 a simple win is 52 Nxf7! Kxf7 53 Bd5.

52 Kg2   Qc3

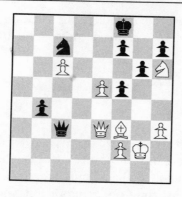

Black now seems to have some chances to save the game, since the exchange of queens is certainly no win for White in view of the bad position of his knight. But once again we see that a piece is still a piece, though for the moment it is badly placed.

53 Qa7!

Less convicing is 53 Nxf5 gxf5 54 Qh6+ Kg8! (54 ... *Ke8 55 Qd6 Ne6 56 c7!*) 55 Qg5+ Kf8, although 56 Qxf5 should suffice for the win. The text introduces a nice final combination.

53 ...	Qxe5
54 Qb8+	Black resigned

After 54 ... Kg7 55 Qh8+! leaves White with an extra piece in the endgame, and 54 ... Ke7 55 Ng8+ leads to mate. A neat finish for an interesting fighting game.

(*June 1975*)

ENDGAMES
UNDER THE
MICROSCOPE

PART III

"EASY WINS" AREN'T ALWAYS EASY!

Shamkovich vs. Liberzon; Ruy Lopez
Moscow Jubilee Tournament, 1967

Moscow chess organizers celebrated the fiftieth anniversary of the Soviet Union by putting together a fine "Jubilee" tournament (not to be confused with the Moscow International tournament the same year). This event comprised twelve participants: eight experienced grandmasters—among them former World Champion Smyslov, Bronstein, Polugaevsky, Simagin, and Lilienthal—and four young masters.

Here is an interesting game from the tournament with a very crucial rook ending.

White: Leonid Shamkovich
Black: Vladimir Liberzon

Ruy Lopez

1	e4	e5
2	Nf3	Nc6

3	Bb5	a6
4	Ba4	Nf6
5	0-0	Be7
6	Re1	b5
7	Bb3	0-0
8	c3	d6
9	h3	Nb8

A great many modern tournament games open with dry repetitions of well-analyzed variations some fifteen or twenty moves deep, and the players don't use their own heads until the second half of the game. Is this progress? Has chess reached such an advanced stage that avoiding well-known opening lines is tantamount to obtaining an inferior game? Has the opening phase become a mere choosing among prescribed systems?

No, opening theory has not yet killed the genius of the creative player. From a purely tactical standpoint, it often makes sense to choose fashionable opening systems, since they are the ones most analyzed by players and theoreticians and most discussed in the chess literature.

But there are other lines. Although some may not be as good as the fashionable ones, others may be even better. I think the art of chess would be better served by the use of a wider range of openings in tournament play. Look at some of the old tournament and theory books and see how many interesting lines of play there were in some openings, many of them quite forgotten today.

10	d4	Nbd7
11	Bg5	

This, at least, is a change from the usual 11 Nbd2, etc. And look, White soon gets some advantage!

11 ...   Bb7
12 Nbd2   c5
13 Bc2

White wants to bring his knight to e3 or g3 via f1, so he first protects his e-pawn.

13 ...   h6

This move is a matter of taste. It certainly isn't bad, but 13 ... Re8 and 13 ... cxd4 14 cxd4 Re8 also have their merits.

14 Bh4   Re8

But here 14 ... Nh5 is the logical move. The simplification 15 Bxe7 Qxe7 16 Nxe5 dxe5 17 Qxh5 cxd4 18 cxd4 Rac8 followed by 19 ... exd4 is certainly not to be feared.

15 Nf1   Nh7

I don't like this move. Again, 15 ... Nh5 is right.

16 Bg3   Ng5

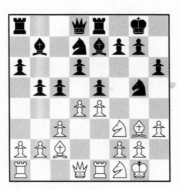

17 dxe5!

Simple and good. White now gets a slightly better position.

| 17 . . . | Nxf3+ |
| 18 Qxf3 | Nxe5 |

The alternative 18 . . . dxe5 19 Rad1 does not look pretty. White already has an edge.

| 19 Qh5 | g6 |
| 20 Qe2 | Bf6 |

If Black does nothing, his position will remain inferior. His d-pawn is weak, White has complete control of d5, and—most important—Black has no effective counterplay.

Black should therefore be looking for tactical chances. One possibility is 20 . . . Bh4, and if 21 Bh2 Black can try the complicated push 21 . . . d5. Also 20 . . . Qa5 offers better chances than the text: it prevents 21 Rad1 and prepares an eventual . . . b4.

21 Rad1	Bg7
22 Ne3	Qe7
23 Nd5	

Positionally good enough, but 23 Qd2 is even more promising, with the idea of replying to 23 . . . Rad8 with 24 f4. If then 24 . . . Nc4 25 Nxc4 bxc4 26 f5 with advantage. The pawn sacrifice 24 . . . Nd7 25 Qxd6 Qxd6 26 Rxd6 Nf6 is also insufficient, because of 27 Rxd8 Rxd8 28 Nf1!.

23 . . .	Bxd5
24 Rxd5	Rad8
25 Red1	Nc4

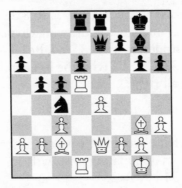

In a positionally difficult situation Black finally decides to seek tactical complications, and he soon has some success. The text move threatens the b-pawn and prepares an eventual ... f5.

26 b3   Nb2

But not 26 ... Na3 27 Bxd6 Qe6 28 e5, etc. The text move prepares a pawn sacrifice to escape into an endgame with good drawing chances.

27 Rc1   c4

After 27 ... Bxc3 28 Bb1 Black has to return the pawn, ending up with a trapped knight.

28 Bb1   Nd3
29 Bxd3   cxd3
30 Qxd3

But not 30 Rxd3 Qxe4 31 Re3 because of 31 ... Qc6.

30 ...   Qxe4
31 Qxe4   Rxe4
32 Rxd6   Rxd6

It's hard to say whether 32 . . . Rc8 33 Rxa6 Rxc3 34 Rxc3 Bxc3 offers better drawing chances; it would seem to, considering that 35 a4 Re1+ 36 Kh2 b4 followed by 37 . . . Rb1 wins the b-pawn. But the text move looks all right.

$$33 \quad Bxd6 \qquad Re2$$

Black's defense would be easier if he first drove the bishop from its dominating post with 33 . . . Re6 and then played 34 . . . Re2.

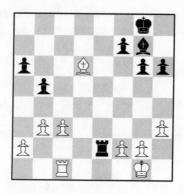

$$34 \quad c4!$$

This pawn is very strong and will cause Black a great deal of trouble.

$$34 \ldots \qquad bxc4$$
$$35 \quad bxc4 \qquad Bb2$$

On 35 . . . Bd4 White can continue 36 c5! Rxf2 37 Kh2 and the c-pawn will win material. But 35 . . . Bf8 36 c5 Bxd6 37 cxd6 Rd2 38 Rc6 a5 is playable.

| 36 Rd1 | Rc2 |
| 37 c5 | Kg7 |

Black is playing with fire. He should take the opportunity to force a rook ending with 37 ... Ba3 38 c6 Bxd6 39 Rxd6 Kg7, with a probable draw. White can try 38 Rd5, which seems to make no difference after 38 ... f6 39 c6 Bxd6 40 Rxd6 Kf7, etc.; but Black should not play 38 ... Rxa2 because of 39 Be5!.

38 g4	f5
39 Kg2	fxg4
40 hxg4	Kf6

This was the last opportunity for 40 ... Ba3 41 Rd5 Kf7, threatening 42 ... Rxa2. Time trouble may have been a factor here.

41 Bf4!

By keeping the bishops on the board, White decisively increases his winning chances in the endgame. Black now has no choice.

41 ...	Rxc5
42 Rd6+	Kf7
43 Rxa6	h5

Black could have made White's task much more difficult with 43 ... Bc1! followed by 44 ... Rc4.

| 44 Be3 | Rd5 |
| 45 gxh5 | gxh5 |

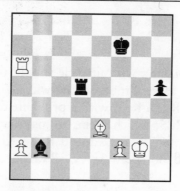

After this recapture Black's problem will be that he can't trade bishops because the rook endgame is lost. But the endgame is probably lost also after 45 . . . Rxh5 46 a4 Rd5 47 Kf3, again because the bishops can't be exchanged. The ending Black has chosen is the most difficult.

46 a4   Bd4

As I mentioned, the rook endgame is lost. After 46 . . . Bc3 White's technical task would be very difficult, if not impossible, to solve.

47 Bxd4   Rxd4
48 a5

In principle, the win is now quite simple for White. He will play his rook to a8, push his a-pawn to a7, and then advance his f-pawn. Black will be forced to capture that pawn on f6 or f7, whereupon White will win with Rf8 + or Rh8.

Black doesn't have time to force the exchange of pawns on the kingside, since after 48 . . . h4 49 Ra8 Rd2 50 a6 h3 + 51 Kxh3 Rxf2 52 a7 Ra2 53 Rh8 he is one tempo too late. His only chance is to bring his king in front of his pawn, to make things difficult for White.

48	. . .	Rg4 +
49	Kf3	Ra4
50	Ra8	Kg6
51	a6	Kg5

52 Ke3

Although after 52 a7 Kh4 Black can hide his king in time, the ending is still a win for White, as follows:

White plays 53 Kg2 Ra2 54 Kg1!, with the idea 54 . . . Ra1 + 55 Kh2 Ra2 56 Kg2! and Black is in zugzwang; e.g., 56 . . . Ra6 57 f4 Ra2 + (otherwise *58 f5*, etc.) 58 Kf3 Ra3 + 59 Ke4 Ra4 + 60 Kd3 Ra3 + 61 Kc4 Kg4 (or *61 . . . Ra4 + 62 Kb3 Ra1 63 f5 Kg4 64 Rg8 + Kxf5 65 a8Q Rxa8 66 Rxa8 h4 67 Rh8 Kg4 68 Kc3 h3 69 Kd3 Kg3 70 Ke2 Kg2 71 Rg8 +* and wins) 62 Rg8 + Kxf4 63 a8Q Rxa8 64 Rxa8 h4 65 Rh8 Kg3 66 Kd3 h3 67 Ke2 and White wins (*67 . . . Kg2 68 Rg8 + Kh1 69 Kf3 h2 70 Kg3 Kg1 71 Kh3 + Kh1 72 Ra8*, etc.).

But Black can put up more resistance with 54 . . . Kh3! (instead of *54 . . . Ra1+*) 55 f4 h4. Now White must play 56 f5, after which Black has two lines of defense:

A) 56 . . . Ra5 57 f6 Ra6 58 f7 Rg6+ 59 Kh1 Ra6 looks quite good, but White's only move is good enough to win: 60 Rg8!.

B) 56 . . . Rg2+ 57 Kf1 Rg7 can also be tried, but this, too, is inadequate: 58 Kf2 Rh7 59 Kf3 Kh2 60 Kf4 h3 61 f6 Kh1 62 Kf5 h2 63 Ke6 and wins.

52 ...		Ra3+
53	Ke4	Ra4+
54	Kf3	

Simpler is 54 Ke5 Ra5+ 55 Ke6 Ra2 56 a7 Kh4 57 f4, threatening to advance the f-pawn. The ending after 57 . . . Kg4 58 Rg8+ Kxf4 59 a8Q Rxa8 60 Rxa8 h4 61 Ra4+ Kg3 62 Kf5 h3 63 Ra3+ Kg2 64 Kg4 h2 65 Ra2+ Kg1 66 Kg3! is an easy win for White.

54 ...		Kh4
55	Ke3	Ra3+

55 . . . Kh3 is no better. White wins with 56 f4 Kg4 57 f5! (but not *57 a7 Ra3+* with continuous checks along the a-file) 57 . . . Ra3+ (or *57 . . . Kxf5 58 a7 Ra3+ 59 Kf2*, etc.) 58 Ke4 Ra4+ 59 Ke5 Ra5+ 60 Ke6 Rxf5 61 a7 Ra5 62 Rg8+ Kf3 63 a8Q Rxa8 64 Rxa8 h4 65 Kf5 and wins.

56	Ke4	Ra4+
57	Kf5	Ra5+
58	Ke6	

White doesn't seem to have found the winning line shown after White's fifty-second move. Although this king maneuver accomplishes nothing, neither does it spoil the win, since the king can always turn back.

58 ...   Kg4

The threat of 59 f4 should be prevented by 58 ... Ra4!. White then wins the ending with 59 a7 Ra6 + 60 Kd5 Ra5 + 61 Kc4 Ra4 + 62 Kd3! Ra3 + 63 Ke2 Ra2 + 64 Kf1 Ra1 + 65 Kg2 Ra2 66 Kg1!, etc., as given above. But White has to see the trap 62 Kb3 Ra1 63 f4 Kg4! with a draw!

59 a7

Now this wins easily. White threatens 60 Rg8 +, and if 59 ... Kh3 60 f4. So Black must check.

59 ...   Ra6 +
60 Ke5

But not 60 Ke7 Kh3 61 f4 Kg4!, etc.
The simplest win here is 60 Kd5. Now 60 ... Ra5 + loses immediately because of 61 Kc6 with the double threats 62 Kb6 and 62 Rg8 +. Black must therefore try 60 ... Kh3, but then 61 f4 Kg4 62 f5!

Kxf5 (or *62 . . . Ra5 + 63 Kc4*) 63 Rf8 + Kg4 64 a8Q
Rxa8 65 Rxa8 h4 66 Ke4 a3 67 Ke3, winning easily.

60	. . .	Ra5 +
61	Ke4	Ra4 +
62	Ke3	Ra3 +
63	Ke2	Ra2 +
64	Kf1	

Maneuvering the king to c4 would win more
quickly here.

64	. . .	Kh3
65	f4	

At last this pawn advances, and it decides the game.

65	. . .	Ra5

Also useless is 65 . . . h4 66 f5 Kh2 67 f6 Ra6
because of 68 Ke2! Re6 + 69 Kd3 and Black is one
tempo too late.

66	Ke2	Ra2 +
67	Kd3	Ra3 +
68	Kc4	Kg4

There is nothing else Black can do about 69 f5.

69	Rg8 +	Kxf4
70	a8Q	Rxa8
71	Rxa8	h4
72	Kd3	h3
73	Ke2	Black resigned

(*March 1968*)

SMYSLOV LOSES A DRAW

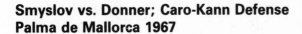

**Smyslov vs. Donner; Caro-Kann Defense
Palma de Mallorca 1967**

It's always a sensation when one of the world's leading grandmasters—a former world champion, no
less—loses a game, even against another grandmaster.
In the 1967 Palma de Mallorca tournament, former
World Champion Smyslov's only loss was against
Donner. Although the Dutch grandmaster was in very
good form in this game, it must be said that Smyslov
played far from his best. But the game was a tough,
interesting fight to the last pawn.

**White: Vasily Smyslov
Black: Jan Hein Donner**

Caro-Kann Defense

1 e4	c6

As a rule, it is not a good idea to play a purely defensive opening like the Caro-Kann or the French against Smyslov. He handles those lines perfectly, usually getting some solid advantages in positions in which it is very difficult for his opponent to defend properly. I think 1 ... e5 and 1 ... c5 are better choices against him.

2	d4	d5
3	Nc3	dxe4
4	Nxe4	Nd7

This is the latest fashion in the Caro-Kann. The Petrosian–Spassky world championship match produced some critical problems for Black in the main line, 4 ... Bf5.

5	Bc4	Ngf6
6	Ng5	

This is probably the most promising line for White. On 6 Nxf6+ Nxf6 7 c3, which prevents 7 ... Bf5 because of 8 Qb3, Grandmaster Filip has found the good answer 7 ... Qc7.

6	...	e6
7	Qe2	Nb6

Black has to pay attention to such tactical threats as 8 Nxf7!. The knight doesn't stand especially well on b6, but it has to go there so that Black can develop his other pieces normally.

8	Bd3	h6

It is well known that Black can't take the pawn: 8 ... Qxd4 9 N1f3 followed by 10 Ne5.

The immediate 8 ... c5 is also inferior, leaving

White with the better game after 9 dxc5 Bxc5 10 N1f3 h6 11 Ne4 Nxe4 12 Qxe4, as in Matulovic–Donner from this tournament.

One gets the impression that Black has just as many problems in this variation as he does after 4 . . . Bf5.

9	N5f3	c5
10	dxc5	Bxc5
11	Ne5	Nbd7

Black still has to be very careful. The immediate 11 . . . 0-0 looks dangerous, since White gets good attacking chances after 12 Ngf3 Nbd5 13 a3 b6 14 g4!, etc. (Darga–Filip, Tel Aviv 1964). In this line, Black can of course try to switch to the variation actually played with 12 . . . Nbd7 instead of 12 . . . Nbd5, but it makes more sense to play this move right away.

12	Ngf3	Nxe5
13	Nxe5	0-0
14	0-0	

Smyslov must have been quite satisfied with the result of the opening. White stands slightly better with a very solid position, and Black has cause to wonder whether he will ever manage to equalize fully. It usually isn't easy to withstand Smyslov's continuous positional pressure in positions like this.

The text move is typical of Smyslov's style. Having forced Black to weaken his king's position (. . . h6), the development 14 Bd2, intending 15 0-0-0 and g4, is probably objectively better. But in fact it gives Black a chance to create great complications with 14 . . . Bd4 15 0-0-0 Qd5, as in Honfi–Pfleger, The Hague 1966. Although it was later found that White had very good attacking chances in that game with 16 f4!, Smyslov is not the kind of player who allows his opponent to get any counterplay. He would rather seek less in the position than allow Black to escape the pressure.

14 ...	b6
15 Rd1	Qe7

Donner points out that 15 ... Qc7 allows 16 Ng4 Nxg4 17 Qxg4, forcing Black to play 17 ... f5. The simple 16 Bf4 is also good.

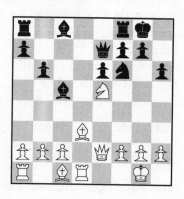

16 b4!

Although it's not quite in Smyslov's style, this is a very good move and promises White more than 16 Bf4 Bb7 17 Bg3 Rfd8, as in Matanovic–Pfleger, Tel Aviv 1964.

Black obviously can't take the pawn because he loses the exchange after 16 ... Bxb4 17 Nc6 Qc5 18 Nxb4 Qxb4 19 Qf3, threatening both 20 Qxa8 and 20 Ba3; e.g., 19 ... Qg4 20 Qxg4 Nxg4 21 Ba3, etc.

16 ...	Bd6
17 Nc6	

This leads to complications that are not entirely clear and that give Black a chance for active counter-play. White has no reason to create these complications and sacrifice a pawn, even if only temporarily, since he can keep all his positional advantages with 17 Bb2 Bb7 18 a3.

17 ...	Qc7
18 b5	Nd5

The continuation 18 ... Bxh2+ 19 Kh1 Bd6 20 Bb2 Nd5 transposes to the game.

19 Bb2	Bxh2+

Black has no choice. Exchanging White's king's bishop makes no sense, since after 19 ... Nf4 20 Qf3 Nxd3 21 Rxd3 Black faces great difficulties if he accepts the pawn sacrifice: 21 ... Bxh2+ 22 Kh1 Bd6 23 Rxd6! Qxd6 24 Ba3 and wins. Black must keep his good knight—it's his only chance to hold the position.

20 Kh1	Bd6
21 Be4	

The easiest way to regain the pawn with a good game. Also worth considering is 21 c4 Nf4 22 Qf3 or 22 Qe3, which leads to a fine game for White after 22 ... Nxd3 23 Rxd3, etc. But Black plays 22 ... Bb7, which just holds the position.

21 ...	Bb7

Black can't keep the extra pawn, since 21 ... Nf4 is met by 22 Qd2. The move 22 c4 was also threatened.

22 Bxd5

22 c4 can be answered by 22 ... Bxc6 23 bxc6 Ne7 or 23 ... Nf4. White's move, removing Black's strongest piece, seems best.

22 ...	exd5
23 Qg4	

The immediate 23 Rxd5 Bxc6 24 bxc6 is also good, since Black can't recapture 24 ... Qxc6 because of 25 Qg4!.

23 ...	f6

24 Qe6 + ?

So far Smyslov has conducted the game very well, and after 24 Rxd5 he would obtain the superior position. Black would be practically forced to reply 24 ... Bxc6, and after 25 bxc6 the threats of 26 Qe6 + and 26 Rad1 would not be easy to meet.

24 ...	Kh8
25 Rxd5	Bxc6
26 bxc6	Bc5!

Now we can see the difference. If White had not checked on move twenty-four, this move would be out of the question because of 27 Rd7, winning the queen. But now the rook move is not playable because of 27 ... Qf4!, with strong threats against the white king.

Smyslov's decision to meet the threats by trading bishops is quite reasonable.

27	Bd4	Bxd4
28	Rxd4	Rac8

On 28 ... Rad8 the continuation 29 Rd7 Qf4 30 Re7! is good enough for equality. After the text, White's simplest choice is probably 29 Rd7 Qxc6 30 Qxc6 Rxc6 31 Rxa7 Rxc2 32 Kg1 Rd8 33 Re1 with excellent drawing chances. Considering Smyslov's time trouble, this was probably his best option.

29	Rd6	Rfe8
30	Qd5	Re5
31	Qd4	

The immediate 31 Qd3 is better, winning an important tempo.

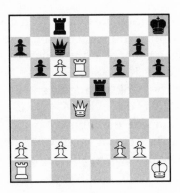

31 ...   Rce8!

Very well played. The threat is 32 ... Re1+ 33 Rxe1 Rxe1+ 34 Kh2 Re6, winning the rook. If 31 ... Rc5 instead, then 32 Re1! gives White serious counterplay after 32 ... Rxc6 33 Rd7, or 32 ... Rxc2 33 Rd7! Qxc6 34 Qg4 Rg8 35 Re8!.

32 f4   Rc5
33 Rd1   Qf7

White's defense would be much more difficult after the simple 33 ... Rxc2 (a move Black would not have had if White had played *31 Qd3*). White may have intended 34 Qd3 Rxc6 35 Rd7 Qxf4 36 Qg6 Rg8 37 Rxg7!, but that beautiful variation is completely refuted by 36 ... Re1+! 37 Rxe1 Qh4+ and mate.

34 Qd3   Qh5+
35 Kg1   Qg4
36 Qf1

This miscalculation must have been caused by time trouble. According to Donner, White would have excellent drawing chances in the endgame after 36 Rd8 Rxd8 37 Qxd8+ Kh7 38 c7 Rxc7 39 Qxc7 Qxd1+ 40 Kf2, but the rook ending after 38 ... Rxc2 39 Qd3+ Qg6 40 Qxg6+ Kxg6 41 Rd7 a5 does not look very promising for White.

The simple 36 Rf1 is a good defending move here, making it very difficult for Black to increase his initiative.

36 ...   Re2?

Donner thought 36 ... Rxc2 was bad because of 37 Rd8 Rxd8 38 Rxd8+ Kh7 39 Qd3+ Qg6 40 Rh8+ and wins. But Black has the better reply 37 ... Qe6!, putting an end to White's attacking attempts.

After the erroneous move in the game, the chances will soon be equal again.

37 R6d2   Rxd2
38 Rxd2   Rxc6

A draw could be agreed here. Donner recommended 38 ... Qc8 instead of the move played, but it makes no essential difference. After 39 Rd7! Qxc6 (taking either pawn with the rook loses to *40 Qd3!*) 40 Qd3 f5 41 Qd4 Qg6 42 Rxa7 Rxc2 43 Ra8+ Kh7 44 Qd5 Black's winning chances are practically nil.

39 Rd8+   Kh7
40 Qd3+   f5
41 Rd5?

Smyslov, probably unaware that the time control has been passed, makes a mistake that leads to a difficult game for him. The obvious 41 Qd5! forces perpetual check.

41 . . .	Rg6
42 Qd2	Re6

This is a loss of time that allows White to get his rook to a better position. Donner rightly considers 42 . . . h5 the correct continuation.

43 Re5	Rc6

In the queen ending after 43 . . . Rxe5 44 fxe5, White's passed pawn would seriously hamper Black's winning chances.

44 Qd3?

I consider this the decisive mistake, leading to a very difficult rook ending for White. He must take a chance here and give his rook more activity with 44 Re8!, threatening Qd5 or Qd8 in some variations. Black would then have only minimal winning chances, if any at all.

44 . . .	Rg6

Donner does not immediately see the point and repeats moves, and the decisive mistake is repeated as well.

45 Qd2	Rc6
46 Qd3?	Qxf4!

This is the point. Black brings the game to a rook ending in which he has excellent winning chances.

47 Rxf5	Qc4
48 Rf7 +	

White's best chance; otherwise he loses another pawn.

48 ...	Qxd3
49 cxd3	a5

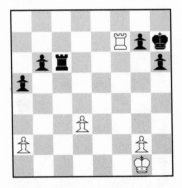

This is a very difficult ending for White. Not only is he a pawn down, but all his remaining pawns are isolated and very weak, his king cannot abandon the g-pawn, and Black has pawn majorities on both wings. Black's immediate threat is 50 ... Rd6, so White's move is practically forced.

50 Rd7	a4
51 Ra7	b5
52 Rb7	Rd6?

It's hard to understand why Donner exchanges his good b-pawn for his opponent's main weakness. By playing 52 ... Rc5 first, threatening 53 ... Rd5, then after 53 Kf2 Black could bring his king into play, protecting his g-pawn with ... Rg5 when necessary. It would then be extremely difficult, perhaps impossible, for White to save the rook ending. Now, on the contrary, it looks more and more like a draw.

53	Rxb5	Rxd3
54	Rb2	Ra3

It makes no difference whether or not Black plays this unnecessary move. Also after 54 ... a3 55 Rc2, White can get his rook behind the a-pawn; e.g., 55 ... h5 56 Rc5 Kh6 57 Ra5, etc.

55	Kh2	h5

56 g3?

Opening the second rank is suicide. Now White's rook can never leave this rank without giving up the a-pawn.

Smyslov was probably worried about ... h4 followed by ... g5, ... Rg3, ... a3, and the journey of the black king to the queenside. But that would not have been as bad as the opening of the second rank. Let's look at a likely possibility.

White begins by simply waiting, 56 Rd2. There could follow 56 ... h4 57 Rc2 g5 58 Rd2 Kg6 59 Rc2 Kf5 (59 ... g4 60 Rc4 leads to nothing) 60 Rc5+ Kf6 61 Rc2 Rg3 (otherwise Black's king can't leave the g-pawn) 62 Rc4 a3 63 Re4! Kf5 64 Re8 Kf4 65

Re7 Re3 66 Ra7, and it is not to be seen how Black can improve his position.

White seems to have sufficient defending resources by cutting off the black king on the d-file; for instance, 66 ... Rc3 67 Rf7+ (even simpler is 67 Ra4+) 67 ... Ke4 68 Rg7 Rg3 69 Rd7. It seems Black can make no further progress unless he is willing to trade his g-pawn for White's a-pawn ... but in that case the ending should be a draw.

Anyway, passive waiting here was the only way to give White chances to fight for a draw. Now he has a lost ending.

56 ...		g5
57 Kg2		

If White starts checking, Black brings his king to f3 via g4. But now the threat of 58 Rb7+ can be annoying.

57 ...		Rd3
58 Rb4		

A desperate decision, but now even passive defense is hopeless. Black would proceed according to the following plan: first push ... a3, then approach with the king; when White tries to cut it off with Rf2, Black threatens ... Rd1-b1-b2. Once Black has his king centralized, he carries out the threat of bringing his rook to b2, winning easily.

The text gives up the a-pawn at once but allows White's piece more freedom of action, thus creating more technical difficulties for his opponent. But this is already a book win.

58 ...		a3

It makes no essential difference whether Black plays

this first or takes the pawn immediately with . . .
Rd2 + and . . . Rxa2.

	59 g4	hxg4

This is certainly the simplest, but Donner says 59
. . . h4 is more exact. In that case Black has to avoid
stalemate after 60 Ra4 Rd2 + 61 Kh3 Rxa2? 62
Ra7 + Kg6 63 Ra6 + Kf7 64 Rf6 + !, etc. But Black
wins after 60 Ra4 Rg3 + 61 Kf2 Kg6 62 Rb4 Kf6 63
Re4 Kf7 and the king comes through because of
White's zugzwang.

60	Rxg4	Kg6
61	Ra4	Rd2 +
62	Kg3	Rxa2
63	Ra5	

63 Kg4 is pointless, since after 63 . . . Ra1 the king
is forced back because of the threat 64 . . . a2.

63 . . .	Ra1

This is a book win, so from this point we will rely
on analysis by Averbakh in his books on the endgame.

64 Kg2	Kf6
65 Kh2	g4!

But not 65 ... Ke6? 66 Rxg5 Ra2+ 67 Kh3 Rb2 (the threat was *68 Rg3*) 68 Ra5 a2 69 Kg3 Kd6 70 Kf3 Kc6 71 Ke3 Kb6 72 Ra8 Kb5 73 Kd3 Kb4 74 Rb8+ and draws.

66 Ra4	Ke5
67 Rxg4	Ra2+!

This check is essential, since 68 Rg3 was threatened. After 67 ... Rb1 68 Ra4 Rb2+ 69 Kg3 a2 70 Kf3 White draws easily.

68 Kh3

The last hope: 68 ... Kd5? 69 Rg3! and White draws. But now White's king is too far from the pawn.

No better is 68 Kg3, when Black proceeds 68 ... Kd5; e.g., 69 Ra4 (*69 Rf4 Rb2 70 Ra4 a2*, and White is one tempo too late) 69 ... Kc5 70 Kf3 Kb5 71 Ra8 Kb4 72 Rb8+ (or *72 Ke3 Rh2*, etc.) 72 ... Kc3 73 Rc8+ Kd2 74 Ra8 Kc1 75 Kg3 (or *75 Ke3 Rh2*) 75 ... Ra1 76 Rc8+ Kb2 77 Rb8+ Ka2 followed by 78 ... Rb1 and Black wins easily.

68 ...	Rb2
69 Ra4	a2
70 Kg3	Kd5
71 Kf3	Kc5
72 Ke3	Kb5
73 Ra8	Kb4

White resigned

An instructive game with many interesting moments.

(July 1968)

THE ROAD NOT TAKEN

**Tal vs. Korchnoi; Queen's Indian Defense
Semifinal Candidates' Match, 1968**

Right now chess fans the world over are giving most of their attention to the matches among the candidates for the world title. Although the matches include a number of good fighting games, there are also many mistakes that are hard to understand in such high-level competition. Certainly these matches are a great strain on the players' nerves, but that is no excuse for some of the serious blunders we have seen. Alekhine and Capablanca had nerves, too!

One of the most interesting problems arose in the first match game between Tal and Korchnoi, which featured a pawn endgame—a rare guest in modern competition and a most instructive one.

The crucial position arose after the following moves:

White: Mikhail Tal
Black: Victor Korchnoi

Queen's Indian Defense

1 d4 Nf6 2 c4 e6 3 Nf3 b6 4 g3 Bb7 5 Bg2 Be7 6
0-0 0-0 7 Nc3 Ne4 8 Qc2 Nxc3 9 Qxc3 c5 10 Be3 Bf6
11 Rfd1 Bxf3 12 Bxf3 Nc6 13 Bxc6 dxc6 14 Qd3
cxd4 15 Bxd4 c5 16 Bc3 Qe7 17 Qd7 Rfd8 18 Qxe7
Bxe7 19 e4 h5 20 Kf1 Bf6 21 Bxf6 gxf6 22 Ke2 Kg7
23 Rxd8 Rxd8 24 Rd1 Rxd1 25 Kxd1 Kg6 26 Ke2
Kg5 27 Kf3 f5

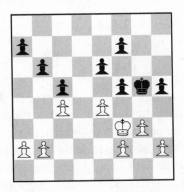

Tal now played 28 h3?, and the game was eventually drawn.

But undoubtedly the most plausible and interesting
continuation is 28 e5!. There were many heated de-
bates about the possible outcome of the game after
that move, and finally Grandmasters Smyslov and
Furman almost simultaneously published deep anal-
yses proving that 28 e5 would have won. It is another
question whether Tal could actually have won with
that move in a practical game, since the winning variations are extremely exhaustive and complicated. It

should be noted too that the defense would have been no less difficult for Korchnoi.

The endgame resulting from 28 e5 will no doubt be of great interest to chess lovers, and the main winning lines as worked out by Smyslov and Furman, which I will now explain, are instructive and of practical value. The actual conclusion of the game (*28 h3*, etc.) follows this analysis.

After 28 e5, it is best for Black not to disturb the pawns on the queenside for the time being. He must therefore choose between 28 ... f6 and 28 ... h4. These two main lines are analyzed separately.

I. 28 ... f6

29	h4+	Kg6
30	Kf4	

White now has certain advantages. His king is actively posted, he has an extra tempo-move with his queenside pawns, and—given the right circumstances—he may be able to get a distant passed pawn on the kingside with f3 and g4. For instance, 30 ... fxe5+ 31 Kxe5 Kf7 32 f3 Ke7 33 g4 fxg4 34 fxg4 hxg4 35 Kf4 is an easy win for White.

If Black remains passive, he will soon get into zugzwang, as the following possibilities show: 30 ... Kf7 31 f3 Kg6 32 a3! (but not *32 g4? fxg4 33 fxg4 fxe5+ 34 Kxe5? hxg4 35 Kf4 Kh5!*, etc.) 32 ... a6 33 a4 a5 34 b3 Kf7 35 g4 fxg4 36 fxg4 hxg4 37 exf6 Kxf6 38 Kxg4 and wins.

But Black has a good defense.

30 ...	a6!

Now White must be careful not to get into zugzwang himself. If he prevents 31 ... b5 with 31 a4, there follows 31 ... Kf7 32 f3 Kg6 33 b3 a5 and White is in zugzwang. The same thing happens after 31 f3 b5 32 cxb5 axb5 33 a3 c4, or 33 b4 c4.

31 a3!

The only correct move. White must keep his b-pawn on its original square to have the tempo-move b2-b3 available.

31 ...   b5

If Black does not take this chance he will be zug-zwanged as in the note after White's thirtieth move: 31 ... Kf7 32 f3 Kg6 (or *32 ... b5 33 cxb5 axb5 34 g4 fxg4 35 fxg4 fxe5+ 36 Kxe5 hxg4 37 Kf4 and wins*) 33 a4 a5 34 b3, etc.

32 cxb5

Not 32 b3 bxc4 33 bxc4 a5 34 a4 Kf7 35 f3 Kg6 and White is in zugzwang. Or 32 f3 bxc4 33 a4 a5 and it's zugzwang for White again.

32 ...   axb5
33 b3!

Position after 33 b3! (analysis)

The character of the position has changed some-what. White has a chance to create a very strong distant passed pawn on the a-file; Black, meanwhile, can keep White's king busy with the threat of . . . c4. As we will see, White holds the higher trumps.

Once again Black must choose between two lines: either passive defense with 33 . . . Kf7, or liquidation of the tension with 33 . . . fxe5 +. We will examine each possibility in turn.

A.

33 . . .   fxe5 +

This plausible move certainly creates the most dif-ficulties for White. Now the following continuation looks all right for Black: 34 Kxe5 Kf7 35 b4 (not *35 a4 c4!* or *35 f3 Ke7 36 g4? fxg4 37 fxg4 hxg4 38 Kf4 c4*) 35 . . . c4 36 Kd4 e5 + 37 Kc3 Ke6 38 a4 bxa4 39 Kxc4 Kd6 40 b5 a3 with equality.

34 Ke3!!

Position after 34 Ke3 (analysis)

34 . . .   f4 +

This is the kind of move we see in endgame studies! White now gets a winning position, since his opponent will not be able to cope with the very strong distant passed pawn on the a-file. White will operate with passed pawns on both flanks to achieve his aim.

If Black tries to catch the a-pawn with 34 . . . Kf6, then after 35 a4 we arrive at variation B (see below). After 34 . . . e4 35 a4! Black is one move too late: 35 . . . c4 36 axb5 cxb3 37 Kd2 e5 38 b6 f4 39 b7 e3+ 40 fxe3 fxe3+ 41 Kxe3 b2 42 b8Q, etc.

35 gxf4	exf4+

The same position occurs after 35 . . . Kf5 36 fxe5 Kxe5 37 a4 c4 38 a5 cxb3 39 Kd2 Kd5 40 Kc3 Kc5 41 Kxb3 e5 42 f3, and Black is in zugzwang.

36 Kxf4	Kf6
37 Ke4	Ke7
38 a4	c4

Quite hopeless, of course, is 38 . . . bxa4 39 bxa4 Kd6 40 Kd3, etc.

39 a5!

After 39 axb5 cxb3 40 Kd3 Kd6 41 Kc3 Kc5 42 Kxb3 Kxb5, Black draws easily.

39 . . .	cxb3
40 Kd3	Kd6
41 Kc3	Kc5
42 Kxb3	e5
43 f3!	

Only this extra tempo-move enables White to win the ending. If it were now White's move, the position would be only a draw: 44 Ka3 b4+ 45 Kb3 Kb5 46 a6 Kxa6 47 Kxb4 Kb6. But since it is Black's move,

Black is in zugzwang and must lose after 43 ... b4 44 a6 Kb6 45 Kxb4 Kxa6 46 Kc5, etc.

B.

33 ...   Kf7

Position after 33 ... Kf7 (analysis)

This passive defense leads at best to positions similar to those in variation A above, since Black will be forced to capture on e5.

34 Ke3!

Of course not 34 a4 c4!, etc., and also insufficient to win is 34 exf6 Kxf6 35 Ke3 Ke5 36 a4 because of 36 ... c4! 37 a5 cxb3 38 Kd3 Kd5 39 Kc3 e5 40 Kxb3 Kc5 41 Ka3 b4+ 42 Kb3 (or *42 Ka4 Kc4 43 a6 b3* with a drawish queen ending) 42 ... Kb5 43 a6 Kxa6 44 Kxb4 Kb6 with a draw.

34 ...   fxe5
35 a4   bxa4

After 35 ... Ke7 36 axb5 Kd6 (or *36 ... e4 37 Kf4* threatening *38 Kg5*, etc.) 37 f3 Kc7 38 g4 fxg4 39 fxg4 White's passed pawn on the kingside wins.

```
36 bxa4        Ke7
37 Kd3
```

The old plan 37 f3 is no good anymore: 37 ... c4!
38 a5 Kd6 39 g4 (or *39 Kd2 e4*, etc.) 39 ... fxg4 40
fxg4 hxg4 41 h5 g3 42 h6 g2 43 Kf2 c3 and Black has
nothing to fear.

```
37 ...         Kd6
38 Kc4         Kc6
39 a5          f4
```

Black is one move too late in the variation 39 ...
e4 40 a6 e5 41 a7 Kb7 42 Kxc5 f4 43 gxf4 exf4 44
Kd4 e3 45 fxe3 fxe3 46 Kxe3 Kxa7 47 Kf4 Kb7 48
Kg5 Kc7 49 Kxh5 Kd7 50 Kg6 Ke7 51 Kg7!, etc.

```
40 gxf4        exf4
41 a6          f3
```

After 41 ... e5 42 a7 Kb7 43 Kxc5 e4 44 Kd4 the
position is the same as that in the note after Black's
thirty-ninth move.

```
42 a7          Kb7
43 Kxc5        Kxa7
```

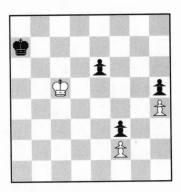

White is now a pawn down, but his more active king position guarantees him the better chances. The question now is which of the black pawns to attack first, the e-pawn or the f-pawn. As we will see, only one of these alternatives leads to a win for White.

44 Kd6!

This wins. Only a draw results from 44 Kd4? Kb6 45 Ke4 Kc5 46 Kxf3 Kd4 47 Kf4 e5 + 48 Kg5 Ke4 49 Kxh5 Kf3 50 Kg5 Kxf2 51 Kf5 Kf3! 52 Kxe5 Kg4, etc.

44 . . .	Kb6
45 Kxe6	Kc7
46 Kf5	Kd6
47 Kf4!	

But not 47 Kg5? Ke5 48 Kxh5 Kf5! 49 Kh6 Kg4 50 h5 Kh3 51 Kg5 Kg2 52 h6 Kxf2 53 h7 Kg2 54 h8Q f2 and Black draws!

47 . . .	Ke6
48 Kxf3	Kf5
49 Ke3	

The win is much more complicated after 49 Kg3 Ke4 50 f3 + Ke3 51 Kg2 Kd4 52 Kh3 Kd3 53 Kh2! Kd4 54 Kg2, etc.

49 . . .	Kg4
50 f4	Kxh4
51 Kf3!	Kh3
52 f5	

White wins easily.

II. 28 . . . h4

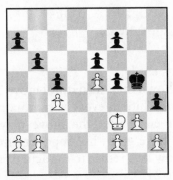

Position after 28 . . . h4 (analysis)

Black tries to secure the g5-square for his king, but the following analysis shows that this cannot be accomplished.

    29 h3   a6
    30 a3!

Again White must be very careful with his pawn moves on the queenside. If 30 a4? a5 31 b3 Kg6! 32 Kf4 Kh5 and White is in zugzwang. As in Variation I, 30 a3 is the right move.

    30 . . .   b5

Black has no adequate defense. 30 . . . a5 31 a4 Kg6 32 Kf4 Kh5 33 b3 leaves him in zugzwang; e.g., 33 . . . Kh6 34 g4! Kg6 35 gxf5 + exf5 36 f3, or 33 . . . hxg3 34 fxg3 Kg6 35 g4 fxg4 36 Kxg4, in either case with an easy win.

    31 cxb5   axb5
    32 b3   b4

White was threatening 33 Ke3 followed by 34 a4.

```
33  a4        c4
34  Ke3       cxb3
35  Kd2
```

White wins easily.

We have shown that the natural move 28 e5! would have won for White in every variation, at least theoretically. But even after the move played, 28 h3?, White could have given his opponent many difficult problems. Now let's return to the actual game (see diagram on page 213).

```
28  h3?       Kf6
29  Kf4       e5 +
30  Ke3       a6
```

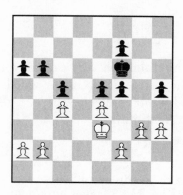

At this point Tal made another mistake by playing 31 b3? Ke6 32 exf5 + Kxf5 33 f3 Ke6 34 g4 f5! 35 gxf5 + (only a draw results from 35 gxh5 Kf6 36 Kf2, since Black would not play 36 . . . Kg5? 37 f4 + ! and wins, but 36 . . . Kg7! 37 Kg3 Kh7 38 Kh4 Kh6 and White is in zugzwang: after 39 a3 b5 White achieves nothing with 40 cxb5 axb5 41 Kg3 because of 41 . . . f4 + 42 Kf2 c4 43 bxc4 bxc4 44 a4 c3 45 Ke2 e4!, etc.) 35 . . . Kxf5 36 h4 Kf6 37 Ke4 Ke6 38 a3 b5 39 cxb5 axb5 40 Kd3 Kd6, and the game was abandoned as a draw.

Instead of 31 b3? in the last diagram, Tal could have given his opponent much more trouble with 31 a3!. Let's take a look at the consequences of this move.

31 a3!	Ke6
32 exf5+	Kxf5
33 f3	f6!

Black cannot rely on the defense chosen by Korchnoi in the actual game, since after 33 . . . Ke6 34 g4 f5, White wins with 35 gxh5! Kf6 36 Kf2 Kg7 (36 . . . Kg5? 37 f4+! exf4 38 Kf3 and wins) 37 Kg3 Kh7 38 Kh4 Kh6 39 a4 a5 40 b3!, and Black is in zugzwang. The text is Black's best defensive chance.

34 g4+	

There is nothing better for White. After 34 a4 a5 35 b3, Black must move, but 35 . . . Ke6 36 g4 f5! leads to a drawish position similar to the actual game.

34 . . .	hxg4
35 hxg4+	Kg6
36 Ke4	

An immediate draw results from 36 f4 f5!.

36 . . .	Kg5!

The only move to hold the position. White wins after 36 . . . Kg7 37 Kf5 Kf7 38 a4 a5 39 b3 Ke7 40 g5 fxg5 41 Kxe5, etc. Now White achieves nothing with 37 Kd5 Kf4, so he must try to reach this position but with Black to move.

37	a4	a5
38	b3	Kg6
39	Kd5	Kg5
40	Ke6	

On 40 Kc6 Kf4 41 Kxb6 Kxf3 Black's pawn queens first.

40	...	Kg6
41	Ke7	

Position after 41 Ke7 (analysis)

Black has a tough choice to make: Should the king go to g5 or to g7? As we will see, only one of those squares is correct.

                    41 ...   Kg7!

Black gets a lost ending after 41 ... Kg5 42 Kf7 f5 43 gxf5 Kxf5 44 Ke7 Kg5 (hopeless is *44 ... e4 45 fxe4+ Kxe4 46 Kd6* and White comes first) 45 Kd6 Kf5 46 Kd5! Kf6 (or *46 ... Kf4 47 Ke6*, etc.) 47 Kc6! Kf5 48 Kxb6 Kf4 49 Kxa5 Kxf3 50 Kb6 e4 51 a5 e3 52 a6 e2 53 a7 e1Q 54 a8Q+ and the queen ending is an easy win for White.

42 Ke8	Kg6

After 42 ... Kg8? 43 Kd7 Kg7 44 Kc6 White will come first.

43 Kf8	Kh6

But not 43 ... Kg5 44 Kf7 and Black is in zugzwang.

44 Kf7	Kg5
45 Ke7	

White's king maneuver has achieved nothing, so he must look for another way. He cannot play 45 Kg7? because of 45 ... f5 46 gxf5 Kxf5 47 Kf7 e4 48 fxe4+ Kxe4 and Black comes first.

45 ...	Kg6

Now we have the same position as in the last diagram but with White to move.

46 Ke6	Kg7
47 Kd6	

Also leading to a draw is 47 Kf5 Kf7 48 f4 exf4 49 Kxf4 Kg6, or 48 g5 fxg5, etc.

47 ...	Kh6
48 Kc6	Kg5
49 Kxb6	Kf4
50 Kxc5	

No better is 50 Kxa5 Kxf3 51 Kb6 e4 52 a5 e3 53 a6 e2 54 a7 e1Q 55 a8Q+ Kxg4 with an easy draw.

50 ...	Kxf3
51 Kb5	e4

52	c5	e3
53	c6	e2
54	c7	e1Q
55	c8Q	

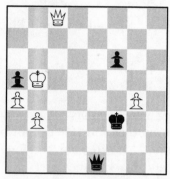

Position after 55 c8Q (analysis)

This is the maximum that White could have obtained from the position before he played the inferior 31 b3. Although it will be very difficult for White to capitalize on his extra pawn, his practical winning chances are good because the onus of precise defense is on Black. In any case, 31 a3 is the line he should have chosen.

(December 1968)

CAN TWO KNIGHTS BEAT A BISHOP?

Keres vs. Ivkov; Ruy Lopez
U.S.S.R. vs. Rest of the World, 1970

It is hard to imagine a more interesting encounter than the "Match of the Century"—officially known as U.S.S.R. vs. the Rest of the World. For this event, which was held in Belgrade, Yugoslavia, in March and April 1970, the U.S.S.R. Chess Federation sent its ten best grandmasters to compete against the ten best grandmasters in the rest of the world, selected by former World Champion Max Euwe. As far as I know, this was the first event in history in which the twenty best players in the world were all together in one place.

It is not appropriate for me to discuss here the results of the event or to praise or criticize the play of my colleagues—in short matches (each grandmaster played only four games) anything can happen. But I want to thank the Yugoslav Chess Federation and their leading personalities for the splendid organization of this great event. Every one of the participants was enthusiastic about the idea of such a match, and the general opinion was that it should be repeated in the near future.

What follows is one of my games from the match. I am fully aware of its flaws and realize that many better games were played in Belgrade. I chose it, however, because after a not very precisely played beginning we arrived at an extremely interesting endgame. The battle between two knights and a bishop, with pawns on both sides, is so rare that I don't remember having ever encountered it before. It's instructive and interesting enough to justify publishing the game.

White: Paul Keres
Black: Boris Ivkov

Ruy Lopez

1	e4	e5
2	Nf3	Nc6
3	Bb5	a6
4	Ba4	Nf6
5	0-0	Be7
6	Re1	d6

Sometimes it's a good idea to avoid the most common variations in favor of older lines. This allows you to be well prepared in a specific variation while your opponent must try either to remember long-forgotten moves or to solve all the problems over the board.

Ivkov is using that strategy here. In choosing a relatively rare variation of the Ruy Lopez, he has in mind a new continuation that he recently used successfully against Smejkal in Prague. Unfortunately, his innovation does not improve the variation.

    7 Bxc6 +   bxc6
    8 d4   Nd7

This leaves Black with a solid but rather cramped position. The whole variation is quite playable when White has already developed his b1-knight to c3, but in this case, when White has the maneuver Nd2-c4 at his disposal, Black will have problems in the opening. The exchange 8 . . . exd4, leading to a position similar to the Steinitz Defense Deferred, may be relatively safer.

    9 Nbd2   0-0
    10 Nc4   Bf6

This is Ivkov's new idea. Black usually defends with 9 . . . f6 instead of 9 . . . 0-0 so that he can meet 10 Nc4 with 10 . . . Nb6 or 10 . . . Nf8. Now 10 . . . f6 11 Na5 would lead to new problems for Black. The answer 11 . . . Nb8 would be forced, since 11 . . . c5 would be met by 12 dxe5, threatening 13 Qd5 + .

    11 Be3!

A good move, directed against . . . c5. The move 11 Na5 is not so strong because of 11 . . . c5. In the above-mentioned game, Smejkal played 11 c3 a5 12 Qa4 but didn't get very much after 12 . . . exd4 13 cxd4 c5.

| 11 . . . | Qe8 |

It's hard for Black to find a plan for active counterplay. His 8 . . . Nd7 and 10 . . . Bf6 have made it clear that he does not want to exchange on d4. But since he will be unable to enforce either . . . c5 or . . . d5, he will eventually have to take on d4 anyway, leaving him with a slightly inferior position. It doesn't make much difference which moment Black chooses to do it.

12 Qd2	Qe6
13 Qc3	Rb8
14 b3	Re8
15 Na5	

White has obtained a clear positional advantage in the opening, and although this knight move practically forces the exchange on d4, I don't think it's the best move. The knight stands much better on c4. With 15 Rad1 or even 15 h3, White would increase his positional pressure and give his opponent almost no chance to free his game.

15 . . .	exd4
16 Bxd4	

16 Nxd4, with the idea 16 . . . Qxe4? 17 Bd2!, is a mistake because of 16 . . . c5!.

| 16 . . . | c5 |
| 17 Bxf6 | Qxf6 |

On 17 . . . Nxf6 the advance 18 e5! is too strong.

| 18 Qxf6 | gxf6 |

A difficult decision. With this move Black forever prevents White's e5 advance, but in weakening his pawn structure he gives White the obviously better position. On the other hand, 18 . . . Nxf6 19 e5 dxe5 20 Nxe5 would also be very unpleasant in view of the weaknesses on Black's queenside.

19 Nd2	Ne5
20 f4	Ng6
21 g3	Bd7

Black has finally completed his development, but his positional liabilities remain. White intends next to station a knight on d5 or f5.

| 22 Nac4 | Bc6 |
| 23 Ne3! | Kf8 |

The capture 23 . . . Bxe4 costs at least the exchange after 24 Ng4!; e.g., 24 . . . Kg7 25 Nxe4 f5 26 Ngf6, and if 26 . . . Re6 Black loses a piece after 27 Nh5 + Kh6 28 Nef6.

| 24 Kf2 | Bxe4? |

Ivkov falls into an elementary trap, noticing the point too late. Were it not for the interesting endgame that follows, the remaining annotations could have been abbreviated with the usual remark about "technique."

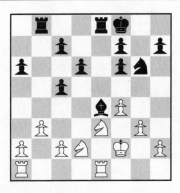

25 f5!

When taking the pawn, Ivkov considered only 25 Nxe4 Rxe4 26 Nd5, which is also very strong and gives White the better endgame. But the text move is stronger still, forcing Black either to give up a piece at once or to retreat his knight to h8, where it would no longer have any value at all.

You may wonder how this game can last so much longer when White already has a piece for two pawns and an almost winning position. The answer is simple. The strain on both players was very great in this important game. One tends to relax a little after gaining an obvious advantage, and of course when you put forth less effort, you produce only second-best moves.

So it was here. I felt that my position was won and would in fact win itself even without precise play. That was a mistake, and, as the continuation shows, it almost cost me a valuable half-point.

25 ...   Bc6

Quite hopeless is 25 ... Nh8 26 Nxe4 Rxe4 27 Nc4, with virtually an extra piece for White.

26 fxg6   fxg6
27 Nec4

Here I should have made a clear plan for the next phase of the game. Logical is 27 c4 followed by the occupation of d5 by one of the knights. After the more-or-less forced exchange on d5, White would have no difficult problems to solve. Instead, I decided to exchange all the rooks. This is not a clearly erroneous plan, but it certainly isn't the best, and it gives Black chances to get some counterplay.

27 . . .   Kf7
28 a3   Rxe1

Otherwise 29 Rxe8 Rxe8 30 b4 would be uncomfortable for Black.

29 Rxe1   g5
30 Ne3   h5
31 Nf5

Though this forces Black to trade the last pair of rooks, it does not improve White's position very much. A better plan is either 31 c4, intending 32 Nd5, or 31 h4. By exchanging too many pieces White risks entering certain types of endgames that are unwinnable with only two knights.

31 . . .   Re8
32 Rxe8   Bxe8
33 h4

A good move, fixing Black's h-pawn on a white square and achieving another endgame advantage. 33 c4 is also good, gaining control of the important square d5.

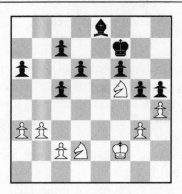

	33 . . .	d5!

Ivkov makes good use of his chances. Now after 34 c4 d4, the threat 35 . . . Bd7 would give White some trouble, especially considering that both players were in time trouble. White therefore decides to secure control of the black squares in the center, but this means more exchanges and better chances for Black to escape.

34	b4	Bd7
35	Ne3	cxb4
36	axb4	gxh4
37	gxh4	Ke6
38	Nf3?	

This is wrong and allows Black to exchange another pair of pawns, which brings him quite close to a draw. Correct is 38 Nb3 Ke5 39 c3, keeping control of d4 and c5 and leaving White with a fairly uncomplicated win. Now the situation becomes extremely critical.

38	. . .	Kd6
39	c3	

This move, made in time pressure, is not the best either. With 39 Ke2 c5 40 bxc5+ Kxc5 41 Kd3 followed eventually by Kc3 and Nd4-b3+, White would have good chances to win the square d4 for his king.

39 ...	c5
40 Ke2	Kc6
41 Kd3	

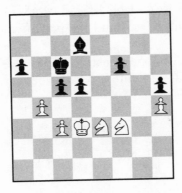

The game was adjourned at this point and Black sealed his move.

The endgame is extremely instructive. Black must remain passive, since the attempt 41 ... d4 42 cxd4 cxb4 43 Kc4 a5 44 d5+ leads to an easy win for White. On the other hand, it isn't easy for White to improve his position. To make progress, he will be forced to capture on c5, but that will reduce the material even more and will leave Black with a potentially dangerous passed pawn on the a-file.

White's control of important central squares still gives him good winning chances, but the matter is by no means clear.

| 41 ... | Be8 |

Apparently the best. Inadequate is 41 ... Kd6 42 bxc5 + Kxc5 43 Nd4 Kd6 (the threat was *44 Nb3 +* followed by *45 Kd4*) 44 Ndf5 + Ke5 45 Ng7, and if now 45 ... f5 46 Nxh5 f4 White gets a won pawn ending with 47 Nxd5! Kxd5 48 Nf6 + and 49 Nxd7, etc.

[The American master Sal Matera pointed out that this "etc." encompasses a studylike endgame: 49 ... Kxd7 50 h5 Ke7 51 h6 Kf7 52 c4 a5 53 h7! Kg7 54 h8Q +! Kxh8 55 c5, and the pawn will queen with check.—Ed.]

Also, 46 ... Bb5 + (instead of *46 ... f4*) 47 Kd2 f4 48 Ng4 + Kf5 49 Nhf6 is hardly adequate to save the game.

42	bxc5	Kxc5
43	Nd4	Bg6 +
44	Kd2	a5

Tactically justified, since 45 Nb3 + Kb5 leads to nothing (*46 Nxd5? Kc4!*). This strong passed pawn gives White a lot of trouble for the rest of the game.

White's only chance to make progress is to try to advance his king. If White's king gets control of the crucial square d4, the game will be won for him in most cases. But as we shall see, solving this technical problem is not easy, if it's at all possible.

[In a letter to "Larry Evans on Chess," a *Chess Life & Review* reader, Brad Willis, suggested that White still wins after 46 ... Kc4 47 Ne7 Kxb3 48 Nxg6 a4 49 Nf4 a3 50 Nd3 f5 51 Nc1 +. Evans continued the analysis with 51 ... Kc4 52 Kc2 f4 53 Nb3 a2 54 Nd2 + Kd5 55 Kb2. Responding several months later,

Grandmaster Keres agreed that this line " . . . is too convincing. Errare humanum est!"—Ed.]

45 Ng2   Kd6!

Best. If at once 45 . . . a4, White has more possibilities after 46 Nf4 Be8 47 Nd3 + ; e.g., 47 . . . Kc4 48 Nf5! Bc6 (48 . . . a3 49 Nd6 + Kb3 50 Nxe8 a2 51 Nc1 +, or 48 . . . Bg6 49 Nd6 + Kb3 50 Nc5 +) 49 Kc2!, or 47 . . . Kd6 48 Nf5 + Kc6 49 Ke3 and White's king gets to d4.

46 Nf4   Be8
47 Nd3

This doesn't spoil anything, but 47 Ke3 a4 48 Nd3 is simpler, forcing the position that appears later in the game.

47 . . .   Bg6
48 Nb5 +   Kc6

49 Nf4?

White cannot afford to trade off one of his knights.

For instance, after 49 Na3 Bxd3 50 Kxd3 the endgame is drawish. The right line, therefore, is 49 Nd4+ Kd6 50 Ke3, as mentioned in the previous note.

When making this move I thought the ending after 49 ... Kxb5 50 Nxg6 Kc4 51 Nf4 d4 52 Nxh5 dxc3+ 53 Kc2 was a win for White. Although further analysis showed that matters were not so simple—e.g., 53 ... a4! 54 Nf4 (after *54 Nxf6? a3 55 Kb1 Kb3* there is no defense against *56 ... a2+* and *57 ... c2*) 54 ... a3 55 Kb1 Kb3—I concluded that White now wins with 56 Ne2.

Black does seem to be lost, but in fact he has a nice way of salvaging his apparently hopeless situation. Let us consider the various possibilities.

Position after 56 Ne2 (analysis)

A) 56 ... a2+ 57 Ka1 f5 58 h5 with an easy win, since 58 ... f4 can be answered simply by 59 Nxf4.

B) 56 ... f5 57 h5! c2+ (*57 ... a2+ 58 Ka1* leads to the previous variation, and *57 ... f4 58 Nd4+ Kc4 59 h6!* also wins easily) 58 Kc1! (*58 Ka1 f4* leads only to a draw) 58 ... f4 (*58 ... a2 59 Nd4+ Kc4*

60 Nxc2 f4 61 h6 f3 62 Kb2! makes no difference) 59
h6 f3 60 Nd4+ Kc3 *(60 ... Kc4 61 Nxc2 f2 62
Ne3+, or 61 ... a2 62 Kb2 leads to already familiar
positions)* 61 h7! f2 *(or 61 ... a2 62 Nxc2 and 63
h8Q+)* 62 Ne2+ Kd3 63 Ng3 a2 64 h8Q and wins.

C) *56 ... c2+!* (the only move that enables Black
to draw with precise play) 57 Kc1 *(57 Ka1 f5 58 h5
f4 is an easy draw)* 57 ... a2! (the only way!—after
57 ... f5 58 h5 White wins as in variation B) 58
Nd4+ Kc4! (but not *58 ... Kc3? 59 Nxc2 f5 60 h6*
and White's pawn queens with check) 59 Nxc2 Kd5!
60 h5 *(or 60 Kb2 Ke4 61 Kxa2 Kf4 and Black draws
after 62 Ne3 f5 63 Kb3 Kxe3 as well as after 62 Nd4
Kg4 63 Nf3 f5 64 Kb3 f4 65 Kc3 Kxf3)* 60 ... a1Q+!
(the final finesse!—after the obvious *60 ... Ke6* White
still wins with *61 Nd4+!* followed by *62 Kb2* and
eventually *Nf5*) 61 Nxa1 Ke6 and draws.

Very fine and beautiful variations. No wonder neither White nor Black could calculate them exactly
during the game with the clocks ticking.

| 49 ... | Be8 |
| 50 Na3 | Kd6 |

Forced, due to White's threat of Ke3-d4.

51 Ke3	Ke5
52 Nc2	a4
53 Nd4!	

Although it looks dangerous to let Black's a-pawn
run, this is safe enough. And it gives Black more problems than the obvious 53 Nd3+ Kf5 54 Kf3 Ke6,
which leads to a position that could arise later.

| 53 ... | a3!? |

It isn't easy to reject a move like this, especially in time trouble, which was afflicting Ivkov at this point. Although Black will lose this pawn, he will achieve further simplification and almost reach a draw.

But only almost. From the practical point of view, 53 . . . Kd6! would give White more trouble, and it's hard to say, even after post-game analysis, whether White could meaningfully inprove his position.

A plausible continuation after 53 . . . Kd6! is 54 Nd3 Bg6 55 Nb2 Be8 56 Nc2 Ke5 (after 56 . . . Bg6 57 Na3 the white king gets to d4) 57 Nd3+ Kf5 58 Kf3 Ke6 (otherwise the king will be pushed back after 59 Nd4+) 59 Ncb4! Kd6 (or 59 . . . a3 60 Nc2 a2 61 Ndb4, winning the pawn) 60 Ke3! and White has made good progress. Whether it is enough to win the game is another question.

<blockquote>
54 Nd3+ Kd6
55 Nc2
</blockquote>

On 55 Nb4 Black has a good defense in 55 . . . Ba4!.

<blockquote>
55 . . . a2
56 Ndb4
</blockquote>

This was White's last move before the time control, and it may not be the best. 56 Na1! seems stronger, threatening 57 Kd4 or even 57 Nb4. After 56 . . . Bb5 White will either win the a-pawn or gain the vital d4 square for his king. If 56 . . . Bg6, White has the pleasant choice between 57 Nb4 (which transposes to the game position) and 57 Nf4 followed by 58 Kd4. Thus White could have avoided much of the trouble he encounters in the game.

56 . . .   Bg6

On his last move before the time control, Black had to decide which way to attack the knight. The other way is also very interesting: 56 . . . Ba4 57 Na1 Kc5 58 Nxa2 Kc4 59 Kd2 leads to the following critical position:

Position after 59 Kd2 (analysis)

Black's best chance is the immediate 59 . . . d4, since 59 . . . f5 60 Nc1 d4 (*60 . . . f4 61 Nd3!*) 61 Ne2! dxc3 + 62 Nxc3 is not adequate because of 62 . . . Kd4 63 Nxa4 Ke4 64 Nc2 Kf4 65 Ne3, etc. On 59 . . . d4, there follows 60 cxd4 Kxd4 61 Nc3. Now the sacrifice 61 ... f5 62 Nxa4 Ke4 63 Nc2 is obviously insufficient, and 61 ... Ke5 is met by 62 Ke3.

But Black still has interesting defensive resources. He can continue 61 ... Bc6! 62 Nc2+ Ke5 63 Ke3 (maybe *63 Ne2!?* is a good idea here) 63 ... Kf5, going after White's last pawn. But this doesn't seem to be good enough: after 64 Nd4+ Kg4 65 Nxc6 Kxh4 66 Kf4! Kh3 67 Nd4!, White threatens to get a theoretically won position with 68 Nf5. If Black avoids that with 67 ... f5, he will be mated after 68 Kf3 Kh4 69 Ne6!, etc. A curious variation!

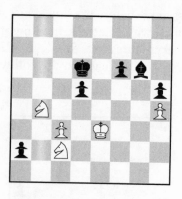

57 Na1	Kc5

Played after long consideration. If 57 ... Bb1 58 Kd4, White wins the d-pawn and then advances his c-pawn. Also insufficient is 57 ... Ke5 58 Nxa2 f5 59 Nb3! f4+ 60 Kf2, and Black can't attack the h-pawn.

With the text, Black hopes for 58 Nxa2 Kc4, but White has a much better continuation ready.

58 Nb3+	Kc4
59 Nd2+	Kxc3
60 Nxa2+	Kb2
61 Nb4	

With the maneuver begun on move fifty-eight White has put the black king out of action. His next task is relatively simple: to win one of Black's pawns without allowing Black to attack his own last pawn.

61	...	Bf7
62	Kd4	Kc1
63	Nf3	Kd1
64	Ke3!	

There is time to get the d-pawn. The main thing is to cut Black's king off from the h-pawn. Certainly there are several ways to win this endgame, but White's seems to be one of the simplest.

64	...	Bg8
65	Nd3	Kc2
66	Nf4	Bf7
67	Kd4	Kd1
68	Kd3!	

Of course not 68 Nxd5? Ke2, etc. The text move places Black in zugzwang—his king must move farther away, after which White can take the d-pawn.

68	...	Kc1
69	Ne2 +	Kb2

69 ... Kd1 70 Nc3 + Kc1 71 Kd4 leads to almost the same position.

70	Nc3	Bg8
71	Kd4	Kc2
72	Nxd5	

Now the pawn can be taken with inpunity. The endgame after 72 ... Kd1 73 Nxf6 Ke2 74 Ke4 is hopeless for Black. White wins the h-pawn and then advances his own h-pawn without giving Black a chance to sacrifice his bishop for it. Ivkov tries one last idea, but it isn't good enough.

72 ...	Bxd5
73 Kxd5	Kd3
74 Nd4	Ke3
75 Nf5 +	Kf4
76 Ke6	Black resigned

After 76 ... Kg4 77 Kxf6 Kf4, the simplest win is 78 Nh6!.

This very rare and fascinating ending justifies publication of the game despite the inaccuracies in the middlegame. There were some tough fights in the "Match of the Century"!

(August 1970, March 1971, September 1972)

"ONLY" A DRAW

Sveshnikov vs. Keres; Two Knights Defense
U.S.S.R. Championship, Moscow 1973

Many chess fans, if not most of them, tend to think of drawn games as likely to be drab and uninteresting. Certainly there are many games like that, especially when the players show no real fighting spirit but give the impression of having tacitly agreed not to harm each other. Fortunately, there are exceptions.

Games can be drawn for various reasons. One is, as I've mentioned, lack of fighting spirit. But when both players are in good fighting form and simply don't allow the opponent to obtain a decisive advantage—this, too, can lead to a draw. Most of us have felt the disappointment of making a blunder that turned a won game into a draw, and the satisfaction of making a draw in a lost position by means of excellent defense.

We may therefore conclude that a drawn game

need not be dull, and in fact can offer as much excitement as many a beautiful win. A case in point is the following draw from the 1973 Soviet Championship, a tough fight almost to the last move.

White: Yevgeny Sveshnikov
Black: Paul Keres

Two Knights Defense

1 e4	e5

My practice of almost always answering 1 e4 with 1 . . . e5 has been criticized because it makes it easier for my opponents to prepare for their games against me. That is true. But I have faith in this reply; I am absolutely convinced that Black has less to fear from possible opening innovations with 1 . . . e5 than with, for instance, many variations of the Sicilian Defense.

2 Nf3	Nc6
3 Bc4	

But this surprised me a little, since nowadays everyone plays 3 Bb5 almost automatically. Should I now invite my opponent into the complicated variations after 3 . . . Nf6 4 Ng5, most of which are almost forgotten? Or is it only I who have forgotten? Maybe my opponent has prepared something!

As I said, I believe in 1 . . . e5, and therefore I must believe that Black can defend successfully after 3 . . . Nf6 4 Ng5. So I rejected the quieter 3 . . . Bc5.

3 . . .	Nf6
4 d4	exd4
5 e5	

This is probably the move that gives Black the most serious problems.

5 . . .	d5
6 Bb5	Ne4
7 Nxd4	Bd7

Which line Black should prefer here is still open to question. For practical reasons probably 7 . . . Bc5 8 Be3 Bd7 9 Bxc6 bxc6 is preferable because it gives White fewer options.

| 8 Bxc6 | bxc6 |
| 9 0-0 | Bc5 |

This and 9 . . . Be7 are considered best, the latter move being the less aggressive choice. Not recommended is 9 . . . c5, depriving the black knight of a potentially important retreat square.

| 10 f3 | Ng5 |
| 11 Be3 | 0-0 |

Though the position looks simple, actually it poses several dangerous problems for Black. His main problem is the weakness of the c5-square: if White establishes a strongpoint there he will have a clear positional advantage. Black must also watch out for the advance f4-f5, which would give White a powerful initiative on the kingside.

Black has some trump cards with which to counter all that. He can try to effect the necessary advance . . . c5, or at least make sure that the c5-square is adequately protected, and on the other wing he can try to play . . . f6 to eliminate White's strong center pawns.

Castling does not help to accomplish either of these plans and it must therefore be considered a serious loss of time. Better is 11 . . . Bb6, removing the bishop from its unprotected position, or even 11 . . . f6 at once can be considered.

| 12 f4 | Ne4 |
| 13 Nd2 | f6! |

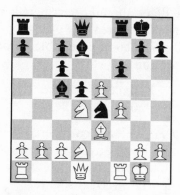

Black must play carefully if he is to equalize. Neither 13 . . . Nxd2 14 Qxd2 f6 15 Nb3 nor 13 . . . Bxd4 14 Bxd4 Nxd2 15 Qxd2 is good enough, since White keeps control of c5. And 13 . . . f5 14 Nxe4 fxe4 (*14 . . . dxe4 15 Nxf5!*) 15 Qd2 leaves White with the better game.

| 14 Nxe4 | dxe4 |
| 15 Qe2 | Bg4! |

The only good move, since 15 . . . fxe5 16 Qc4+ Kh8 17 Qxc5 exd4 18 Bxd4 clearly favors White, and 15 . . . Qe7 or 15 . . . Kh8 leaves White better off after 16 Nb3.

| 16 Qf2 | Qd5? |

Psychologically an interesting moment. For a long time I considered the tempting sacrificial line 16 . . . fxe5!? 17 Nxc6 Rxf4! 18 Nxd8 Rxf2 19 Bxf2 e3 20

Bh4 e2 + 21 Rf2, but I could find no promising continuation. For instance, on 21 . . . Be3 White has the strong answer 22 Be7!, and on 21 . . . h6 he wins an important tempo with 22 Nb7. With an extra rook White should have no trouble repulsing the attack, and so I had to drop that idea.

Having spent a lot of time on that variation, I felt I had to play something quickly—at my age, potential time trouble is my worst enemy! The pawn on c6 had to be protected with either the text move or 16 . . . Qe8, and of course I made the wrong choice, blundering away a pawn. I noticed the blunder as soon as I made my move, but by then it was too late. After 16 . . . Qe8 the chances would have been about equal.

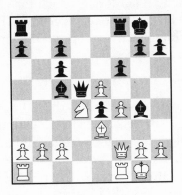

17 Nxc6!

Usually finesses like this work only in blitz tournaments!

17 . . .   Ba3?

Having blundered, I did not like the idea of going into a passive position a pawn down with 17 . . . Qxc6 18 Bxc5 Rf7, etc. The point of this original-looking move is to spoil White's queenside pawn position—but blunders rarely come one at a time!

18 exf6!

After this simple reply Black must lose more material, since 18 ... gxf6 19 bxa3 Qxc6 20 Qg3 costs the bishop. On 18 ... Qxc6 White plays 19 fxg7 first, or after 18 ... Rxf6 19 Ne5 both black bishops are under attack. Not a very pleasant choice for Black!

18 ...   Rxf6

Black is lost. I was concerned mainly with finding a continuation that would allow me to put up further resistance. Probably the best chance is 18 ... Qxc6 19 fxg7 Rf7 20 bxa3 Rxg7, which for practical purposes leaves Black only one pawn down. But the prospect of a White pawn advance on the kingside made this variation unappetizing.

19 Ne5   Qxe5!?

The alternative is 19 ... Bxb2 20 Nxg4 (20 c4? Qxe5!) 20 ... Bxa1 21 Rxa1 Ra6 with only a slight material deficit. But Black would still have a miserable position, especially since his king would be exposed to a strong attack after 22 c3 followed eventually by Bd4 and f5.

Which line should I have chosen? In deciding to enter an endgame the exchange down, my main consideration was that young players like my opponent prefer to attack and usually handle complicated positions with great ingenuity when they have the initiative, but, lacking the technique of a mature grandmaster, they play the endgame with much less assurance. I figured my best chance was to rely on that fact, and the course of the game proves it was the correct decision.

20	fxe5	Rxf2
21	Bxf2	Bxb2
22	Rae1	Bf5
23	Bc5	g6
24	e6?	

This ending is of course easily won for White, who has the material advantage of a full exchange. But from this point on he shows some uncertainty in the selection of a winning plan. Is this because players as a rule become indecisive and sometimes miss the strongest lines the moment they achieve a won position? Or is it that this particular opponent dislikes dull endgames even if they're favorable ones?

Whatever the reason, from now on Black obviously gets more play and makes his opponent's technical task increasingly difficult. With the text move, White allows the exchange of two more pawns, gives up his strong passed pawn, and greatly simplifies the position. The correct line is 24 h3 (*24 g4* at once is also good) 24 . . . h5 (or *24 . . . Bxe5 25 g4 Bd7 26 Rxe4* and the rook penetrates to the seventh rank) 25 g4 hxg4 26 hxg4 Bxg4 27 Rxe4 Bf5 28 Re3, and with the threats of 29 e6 and 29 c3 White wins easily.

	24 . . .	Bxe6
	25 Rxe4	Bxa2

One more enemy pawn eliminated!

	26 Ra4	Bd5
	27 Rxa7	Rc8

Black would like to keep his rook, but this proves impossible. 27 . . . Rxa7 28 Bxa7 c6 was simpler, leading to positions similar to those in the game.

	28 Re1	Bf6
	29 Ra4	Rb8
	30 Rf4	Bg5

To escape immediate loss Black must avoid two things: first, an exchange of bishops; second, the penetration of an enemy rook to the seventh rank. I don't know how I could have parried both those threats after 31 Rg4 Bf6 32 Bd4, but White seems to have other plans.

	31 Rb4	Rd8

Here, of course, 31 . . . Rxb4 is necessary to avoid 32 Rg4, as above. White can still play that, but the move he chooses is also very strong.

	32 Rd4	Bf6
	33 Rd3	c6
	34 Ra3	

The threat of 35 Ra7 now forces Black to offer to trade rooks. But even more convincing is 34 c4! Bf7

35 Rxd8 + Bxd8 36 Ra1, and Black would soon be in a hopeless situation.

                34 ...   Rd7
                35 Ra7

Even more annoying is 35 Ra8 + Kg7 36 Rd1, threatening 37 c4 and 37 Bd4. Time pressure was also a factor for both sides.

                35 ...   Rxa7
                36 Bxa7   Kf7

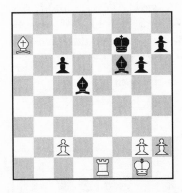

The ending is still won for White, but winning it requires some technical skill on his part. To make progress, he has to work step by step to get his pieces into more active positions. First he must try to exchange bishops—but Black can avoid that. Second, he has to remember the general rule that in the endgame the king is a strong piece and must be brought into action.

But first White makes some noncommittal moves to get past the time control.

                37 Kf2   h5
                38 Rd1   Be5
                39 h3

White does not fear the coming blockade by Black's h-pawn because he hopes to make that pawn an object of attack. But since Black can protect it comfortably, the pawn succeeds in fixing White's g-pawn and tying down the white king. White's task would have been easier after 39 g3.

39 . . .	h4!
40 Be3	Ke6
41 Kg1	Bf6

Black must be very careful about his h-pawn. The threat was 42 Bg5 Bg3 43 Rd4 Ke5 44 Rg4 Be6 45 Ra4, and 41 . . . Kf5 would have been met by 42 Rf1 + Ke4 43 Bg5 Bg3 44 Rf8, etc.

42 Bd4	Be7
43 Re1 +	Kf7
44 Ra1	

The game was adjourned here and White sealed this move.

Black cannot undertake anything but must wait to see what plan his opponent will adopt. Since White can't force the exchange of bishops, he should try to improve the positions of his pieces. He will not be able to make any progress without advancing his king, but just now his king is tied to the defense of the weak g-pawn. Therefore, White's correct plan is to enforce the move g3, which can be done by means of 44 Be5! followed by 45 Kh2 and 46 g3.

Black cannot prevent this. His best chance is to play his bishop to e6 to keep White's h-pawn under attack. But having played g3, White can proceed with h4 and Bg5 and then march his king to Black's g-pawn or c-pawn, depending on which defense Black chooses. Though Black can delay the execution of this plan, he can't prevent it, and in my home analysis I could find no valid defense.

The move sealed by White doesn't spoil anything, but it's a step along the wrong path. White's plan requires him to keep his opponent's king out of play, and for that purpose his rook was ideally posted on e1.

$$44 \ldots \qquad Be4$$
$$45 \ c4$$

This move doesn't seem the best either, since the pawn will be awkward to defend on a white square. 45 c3 is better.

$$45 \ldots \qquad Ke6$$
$$46 \ Ra6 \qquad Kd6$$
$$47 \ Ra5$$

White can't make progress with tactical threats alone. There was still time to think about 47 Kf2 and 48 g3.

$$47 \ldots \qquad Kd7$$
$$48 \ Be3 \qquad Bd8$$

Now the threat of 49 Bg5 has been parried and White has made no headway.

49 Re5   Bf5
50 Bf2   Bf6

On 50 . . . Bd3 White need not play 51 c5 but can continue 51 Re1 (*51 . . . Bxc4 52 Bxh4 Bxh4 53 Re4*).

51 Re1   Be6
52 Rc1

See the note to White's forty-fifth move. The rook plays a passive role protecting the c-pawn, and now Black has a chance to improve the position of his king. And 52 Re4 Bf5 53 Rf4 is not very good because of 53 . . . Ke6 (*54 Bxh4? g5!*).

White's best move is 52 c5. Although Black would get the good square d5 for his bishop, White would no longer have to worry about protecting his c-pawn and it would be harder for the black king to find active play.

52 . . .   Kd6
53 Ba7   Bg5

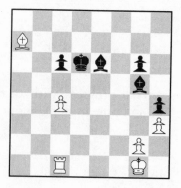

54 Rc3?

Although so far White has not found the best way to realize his advantage, he hasn't spoiled his chances either. But this move is a mistake, allowing Black to bring his king powerfully into play.

Necessary is 54 Rd1+, and if 54 . . . Ke5 55 Bd4+ Kf5 56 Rf1+ Ke4 (or *56 . . . Bf4 57 Be3 g5 58 c5*) 57 Re1+ with a won endgame. Black would have to answer 54 Rd1+ with 54 . . . Kc7, leaving White the choice between 55 c5 or 55 Bf2 Bxc4 56 Bxh4 Bxh4 57 Rd4, etc.

54 . . .	Ke5
55 Kf2	Ke4!

Now that Black has centralized his king he no longer has a lost position, since White's pieces are passively posted and cannot create effective threats. Black threatens 56 . . . Bd2 57 Rc2 Kd3, giving White no time to improve his pawn position on the kingside.

56 Ke2	Bf4
57 Be3	

On 57 Bf2 g5 58 Be3 Black wins a tempo with 58 . . . Be5, and after 58 g3 hxg3 59 Bxg3, simply 59 . . . Bxh3 is playable.

57 . . .	Be5
58 Rc1	Bb2
59 Rc2	Bf6
60 Kd2	

White is trying to bring his king to the queenside to protect his c-pawn and thereby free his rook for action, but Black can easily stop that. On the other hand, if White does nothing, Black can advance his pawns on the kingside, threatening to achieve a draw-ish ending by exchanging them.

The only chance to continue the fight is 60 c5, to free the rook from its defensive duty, but it's a very slim chance. Black can play 60 ... g5, for instance, and if 61 Rd2 Bc4+ 62 Kf2 Be5! (*63 Bxg5 Bd4+ 64 Ke1 Bc3*).

I think White no longer has any winning chances.

60 ...	Bd8
61 Bf2	g5

Preparing the eventual exchange of all the kingside pawns.

62 Kc3	Ba5 +
63 Kb3	Kd3 !

When the game was adjourned on move forty-four I could not have dreamt of such a king! The white pieces are once again pinned to the defense of the c-pawn.

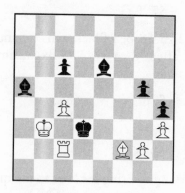

64 Bc5	Bd2
65 Ba3	

On 65 Be7 Black can answer simply 65 ... Bf7, threatening 66 ... Bh5, since the endgame after 66 Rxd2+ Kxd2 67 Bxg5+ Kd3 is a dead draw. But now Black gets the chance to be active on the other side.

65 ...	g4
66 Bc1	Be1

I had a choice here between two drawing lines— and chose the inferior one. I saw that after 66 ... Bxc1 67 Rxc1 g3! Black would have an easy draw due to the latent threat ... Bxh3, and in fact White would have to be careful to avoid getting into a lost position. I thought the line I played was also an easy draw, but I overlooked one small point.

67 Bg5	gxh3
68 gxh3	Bxh3
69 Rc1!	

On 69 Bxh4 Black draws with 69 ... Bg4!. I intended to answer the text move with 69 ... Bg3 70 Bxh4 Bxh4 71 Rh1 Be6 72 Rxh4 c5! with a drawish position, but now I realized that I had completely overlooked 71 Rc3+! and 72 Rxh3, which wins for White.

Too many blunders for one game! Luckily, this last one does not lead to a loss.

69 ...	Ke2!
70 Bxh4!	Bd2

The endgame after 70 ... Bxh4 71 Rh1 Be6 72 Rxh4 Kd3 73 Kb4 is an easy win for White.

71 Rg1	Bf5
72 Bg5	Be1!

Avoiding the last clever trap: 72 . . . Kf2? 73 Ra1! and the bishop is gone (*73 . . . Bxg5 74 Ra5*).

73	Bf6	Be4
74	Bc3	Bf2
75	Rg7	Draw

Since White cannot improve his position, he offered a draw. He can neither force the exchange of bishops nor drive back the black king, and an eventual exchange sacrifice on c6 offers no winning chances.

This interesting game was hardly without flaws, but it was full of fight to the very end.

(June 1974)

LASKER'S EMBARRASSING DISCOVERY

Various Rook Endgames

Everyone recognizes the importance of the endgame. It is there that the advantages accrued in the middle-game are converted to a win and where, generally speaking, creativity matters less than technique. Even minor mistakes can be serious, since there will be no opportunity to make up for them later.

It is simply not possible to become a first-class tournament player without good endgame technique. But technique can be acquired only through hard work, which mostly involves studying dry positions that seem to offer little stimulation for the creative mind. Studying such positions is not a lot of fun for most people; but without proper study it is hardly possible to handle even the simplest endgame positions correctly.

This is where I place the responsibility for the fact that most modern players, even some top grandmas-

261

ters, do not always play the endgame as well as they should. It is no accident that all the world champions and the other great players of history paid special attention to the endgame and achieved the highest standards of excellence in that phase of the game.

Endgame theory is vast, and many thick books are devoted to it. In this article I will deal with only one small part of the theory concerning rook endgames, and I will limit my choice of positions to those with little material.

Though such positions may sometimes appear to be simple, that can be deceptive. Rook endgames are undoubtedly the most complicated endgames of all, with many hidden resources and surprising points. I hope the following few examples will not only demonstrate that fact but will also stimulate interest among all classes of players in this most interesting area of the game.

The theme I have chosen is best illustrated by a world-famous endgame study by Dr. Emanuel Lasker

Dr. Em. Lasker
Deutches Wochenschach, *1890*

White to move and win

that was first published in 1890, when Lasker was twenty-two.

Though the position looks drawish, White forces a win in the following interesting way:

| 1 Kb8! | Rb2 + |
| 2 Ka8 | Rc2 |

White seems to have accomplished nothing. His pawn is attacked and Black's passed pawn threatens to queen, which would produce an immediate draw. A white king move would be answered by a check.

| 3 Rh6 + | Ka5 |

Black's king can't go the b-file because of 4 Kb7 with an immediate win.

4 Kb7	Rb2 +
5 Ka7	Rc2
6 Rh5 + !	Ka4

By repeating his combined king-and-rook maneuver, White has forced the enemy king further down the board. But he still doesn't seem to have achieved anything decisive.

7 Kb7	Rb2 +
8 Ka6	Rc2
9 Rh4 +	Ka3

Black's king is now far enough away to enable White to execute the following decisive maneuver.

10 Kb6	Rb2 +
11 Ka5!	Rc2
12 Rh3 +	Ka2
13 Rxh2	

and wins.

This fine endgame study was widely admired when it was first published. Lasker's maneuver was embarrassingly new to the theory of the rook endgame. Now it is familiar to almost every serious player, and it even turns up occasionally in actual play.

The following position is from my game against Opocensky (White) at the Olympiad in Buenos Aires 1939. Although there are differences between this position and the Lasker study—here Black has an extra pawn and White's rook is trapped in front of the pawn on h7—they are essentially similar. After White's mistake in this position, Black can win by using the Lasker maneuver.

Opocensky–Keres
Buenos Aires Olympiad, *1939*

White moves

1 Kxa4?

The decisive mistake. White can draw by giving up his pawn right away. After 1 Rg8! Black obtains nothing after either 1 . . . Rxh7 2 Rg1+ Kd2 3 Rg2+ Ke1 4 Rc2 Rc7 5 Kb4! a3 6 Rxc3 a2 7 Ra3, or 1 . . . c2+ 2 Ka2! (but not *2 Kxa4? Rxh7*, etc.) 2 . . . Rxh7 3

Rg1+ Kd2 4 Rg2+ Kd3 5 Rg3+ Kd4 6 Rg4+ and Black cannot improve his position.

1 . . .	c2
2 Ka5	

This is the main defensive line. In the actual game, Opocensky played 2 Rg8 and had to resign after 2 . . . Rxh7 3 Kb3 Kb1. The move 2 Ka5 makes things more difficult for Black, but knowing the Lasker maneuver he can enter the following clear winning line.

2 . . .	Kb2

It is interesting to note that with White's rook in front of his pawn, Black has another winning line here, bringing White into zugzwang and winning even more quickly than with the Lasker maneuver: 2 . . . Rh4! 3 Ka6 (of course the king can't go to the b-file) 3 . . . Rh5! 4 Ka7 and now 4 . . . Kb2 5 Rb8+ Ka3 6 Rc8 Rxh7+ wins.

3 Rb8+	Ka3
4 Rc8	Rh5+
5 Ka6	Kb3

All according to the Lasker idea. The threat 6 . . . Rxh7 forces White to check again.

6 Rb8+	Ka4
7 Rc8	Rh6+
8 Ka7	Rxh7+

with an easy win.

There are other examples in which the Lasker maneuver helps to win this type of ending, but let us move on to another question: What if the advanced pawn is not on the c-file or f-file but on one of the central files?

Such endgames seem at first to be hopeless draws. In the Lasker study, for example, if the pawn were on the d-file White would be unable to make progress because Black could check on both the b-file and the c-file and drive the white king too far from the pawn.

But the matter is not so simple: there are many positions in which White has excellent winning chances even with a center pawn. Look at this study.[1]

White moves

The white pawn is already on the seventh rank, but the black pawn is only on the sixth, and this gives White the opportunity to vary his attacking methods. First of all, in many variations he will be able to interpose his rook against White's checks; second, because Black's pawn is only on the sixth rank, White must force the enemy king only to the sixth rank when using the Lasker method.

	1 Kd8	Rd3 +
	2 Kc8	Re3
	3 Rh6 +	Kc5!

The only move. Bad, of course, is 3 . . . Kd5 4 Kd7,

[1]Grandmaster Keres did not identify the composer.—Ed.

etc., and 3 ... Kb5 4 Kd7 Rd3+ allows 5 Rd6!, threatening to queen the pawn with check.

Now, having forced the black king to remain on the c-file, White can execute the Lasker maneuver.

4	Kd7		Rd3+
5	Kc7		

Nothing is gained by 5 Ke8 Re3! and if 6 Rh8 then 6 ... Kd6! is an adequate defense. White must repeat the Lasker maneuver.

5	...		Re3
6	Rh5+		Kb4!

Here 6 ... Kc4 allows White to continue successfully with the Lasker method: 7 Kd7 Rd3+ 8 Kc6 Re3 9 Rh4+ followed by 10 Rxh3 and wins.

7	Kd7		Rd3+
8	Kc6		Re3!

Again the best. With his pawn on the sixth rank, Black cannot play 8 ... Rc3+ because of 9 Kb6 Re3 10 Rh4+ and 11 Rxa3, winning. Now White gains nothing by protecting the pawn with his king, since Black would give check on the d-file.

9 Rh4+!

Presenting Black with an unpleasant choice. His king cannot go to the third rank because of 10 Rxh3, but it will not be happy on the a-file either.

9	...		Ka5
10	Kd6		Rd3+

The threat was 11 Rxh3. The clever trap 10 ... Kb6 11 Rxh3? Rxh3 12 e8Q Rd3+ and 13 ... Re3+, with a draw, is foiled by the simple 11 Rh8!.

11 Kc5!   Re3

Hopeless is 11 ... Rc3+ 12 Kd4 Rc8 13 Rxh3.

12 Rxh3!

and White wins, since 12 ... Rxe7 allows 13 Ra3 mate, and 12 ... Re5+ 13 Kd6 leads to an easy win. A very nice composition.

Now let's look at a position in which White has a center pawn but Black's pawn is already on the seventh rank. The presence of a second white pawn is not essential, as the solution shows.

P. Keres, 1944

White to move and win

This position appears at first glance to be a dead draw. Since White must keep his e-pawn protected by his king (otherwise Black plays ... *Re1*) while his h-pawn plays no role, there seems no way for him to make progress.

One idea is to get the rook to d2 and then to play Kd7 and promote the pawn with e7-e8Q. But this is not so easy, as we will see in the following attempted solution:

| 1 Ra8+ | Kh7 |
| 2 Ra3 | Kh8 |

2 . . . Kxh6 is also possible, of course, but the text is more instructive.

3 h7	Kxh7
4 Rh3+	Kg6
5 Rh2	Kg5

Also good enough for a draw is 5 . . . Kf5 6 Kf7 Kg4, but not 5 . . . Rb1? 6 Rxa2 Rb7+ 7 Kd6 Rb6+ 8 Kd7 Rb7+ 9 Kc6 Rb1 10 Re2! and wins.

6 Rd2	Kf4
7 Kd7	Ke3
8 Rd6	

After 8 e7 Kxd2 9 e8Q Rd1!, White will have to fight for the draw.

| 8 . . . | Rb1! |

and Black draws easily.

As we can see, White must look for a better method if he hopes to win. His first objective must be to get his e-pawn to the seventh rank, which he can achieve as follows:

| 1 Ra7! | Kh8 |
| 2 h7! | |

This places Black in a zugzwang position and allows White to advance his e-pawn. It is interesting that, in the diagram position, if the black king was already on h8 instead of g8 the position would be a draw, since there would be no zugzwang. On the contrary, White would be unable to force his e-pawn forward because of his own zugzwang.

2 ...	Kxh7
3 Ke8 +	Kg6
4 e7	Kh5!

White has achieved his first objective and was threatening to get his rook to the second rank, which would have won easily, as the following variations prove:

A) 4 ... Kg7 5 Ra3 Rb1 (otherwise positions from variations B or C arise) 6 Rxa2 Rb8 + 7 Kd7 Rb7 + 8 Kd8 Rb8 + 9 Kc7 and wins.

B) 4 ... Kh6 5 Ra3 Kh5 6 Rh3 + Kg4 7 Rh2 Kf3 8 Rd2 Kg3 9 Kd7 Re1 10 Rxa2 and wins.

C) 4 ... Kh6 5 Ra3 Kg5 6 Rg3 + Kf4 7 Rg2 Kf3 8 Rb2 Ke3 (White threatened 9 *Kf7*, and 8 ... *Kg3* leads to variation B) 9 Kd7 Rd1 + 10 Kc7 Rc1 + 11 Kb7 and wins.

The idea of Black's text move is to prevent this winning method by bringing his king to the fifth rank at the right time. And it looks as though Black's plan has worked, since now the Lasker maneuver would be ineffective: 5 Ra3 Kh4 6 Kf7 Rf1 + 7 Kg6 Rg1 + 8 Kh6 Re1 and the white king has been driven too far from the pawn. But only now does the really fine play begin, greatly enriching the original Lasker idea.

5 Ra3	Kh4

The only way to prevent the maneuver 6 Rh3 + followed by 7 Rh2, etc. The move 5 ... Kg4 would only shorten the solution.

6 Ra5!

This fine move decides. Black is now in zugzwang and must move his king either to the g-file or to the third rank.

6 . . .   Kg4

6 . . . Kg3 (or . . . *Kh3*) leads to the main line after 7 Kf7.

7 Kf7   Rf1 +
8 Kg6   Re1

Now we see why White had to force the black king to g4; otherwise, 8 . . . Rg1 + would have drawn here.

9 Ra4 +   Kh3!
10 Kf6

The following moves conform to the familiar Lasker method.

10 . . .   Rf1 +
11 Kg5   Rg1 +
12 Kh5   Re1

13 Ra3 +	Kg2
14 Rxa2 +	Kf3
15 Ra7	

In the Lasker study, the fall of the black pawn meant the end of Black's resistance, but here an interesting fight is yet to come.

15 ...	Re6!

This is the point. Now the white king is cut off at the sixth rank and cannot approach the black rook because of the black king. How is White to proceed?

16 Kg5	Ke4
17 Rb7!	

Only this or 17 Rc7 will do it! The natural-looking 17 Rd7 is bad because after 17 ... Ke5 it is White who is in zugzwang.

17 ...	Ke5
18 Rd7!	

Only now does the rook go to d7, placing Black in zugzwang.

18 ...	Ke4
19 Rd1!	Kf3
20 Rf1 +	Ke2
21 Rf7	Ke3
22 Kf5	

and White wins.

Very fine play on both sides, and a fundamental enrichment of the original Lasker idea. It's hard to imagine that there could be so many nice points in such a "simple" endgame position.

The previous examples have by no means exhausted the variations on the Lasker theme. Here's another interesting position.

N. *Kopayev, 1951*
Chess in the USSR, *2nd Prize*

White to move and win

Some similiarity between this study and the previous one is immediately apparent. But there are differences in the solution, as the following analysis demonstrates. For instance, if White begins with 1 Rh8 Rd3 2 Rh5 +, Black answers 2 ... Ka4! and White cannot improve his position. On 3 Kc7 Rc3 + 4 Kd8, Black plays 4 ... Rc2 without fear of a zugzwang position as in the previous study. And 3 Kc7 Rc3 + 4 Kb6 also leads to nothing, since after 4 ... Rb3 + 5 Ka6 Rd3 6 Rh4 + Ka3, White's king is too far from his pawn.

White makes progress as follows.

1 Rf5 +   Ka4
2 Ra5 + !

The point! For the following maneuver to work, Black's king must be driven from a4. Black cannot play 2 ... Kxa5 because of 3 d8Q+ Kb5 (*3 ... Ka4 4 Qh4+*) 4 Qd5+ followed by a check on a2 or d2 and the capture of the h-pawn.

2 ...	Kb4
3 Rh5	Rd3
4 Kc7	Rc3 +
5 Kb6!	

Now the Lasker maneuver functions again. 5 Kd8 Rc2 leads only to a draw.

5 ...	Rd3
6 Rh4+	Ka3
7 Kc7!	

A new point! Nothing is to be gained by the immediate 7 Kc6 Rc3+ 8 Kb5 Rb3+ 9 Ka5 Rd3, since White doesn't have the necessary checking possibilities on the third rank. Before beginning the maneuver he must force the black rook off the third rank.

7 ...	Rc3 +
8 Kd8!	Rc2

Having achieved his aim, White can return to the famous Lasker plan.

9 Ke7	Re2 +
10 Kd6	Rd2 +
11 Kc6	Rc2 +
12 Kb5	Rb2 +
13 Ka5!	Rd2
14 Rh3+	Ka2
15 Rxh2	

and White wins. Very fine!

The Lasker maneuver and its variations make up only one small part of the theory of rook endgames, but they clearly show that even the simplest endgame position can include many points. It makes good sense to pay attention to the endgame!

All that analysis is very nice, very interesting, you may think—but where is the practical value? How often do such positions arise in actual games?

Not very often in master chess, it is true—but they do occur. I can show you two examples from the recent interzonal tournament in Palma de Mallorca, where even the world's leading grandmasters had trouble with some fairly simple rook endgames.

Taimanov–Larsen
Interzonal *1970*

Black to move

This position is a theoretical draw in view of the following continuation, which is held to be the simplest for Black: 1 ... Rg8+ 2 Kf7 Rg4 3 Kf6 Rg8!

and White cannot strengthen his position. But look at what happened in the actual game:

| 1 ... | Kd4!? |
| 2 Ra3 | Ke4 |

As a consequence of 1 ... Kd4, Black obviously cannot prevent the advance of the pawn. Now 2 ... Rg8 + is met by 3 Kf7, when 3 ... Rg4 would be impossible because of 4 Ra4 +.

3 g4	Rg8 +
4 Kh5	Rh8 +
5 Kg5	Rg8 +
6 Kh4	

The game is still a draw. Black has only to play 6 ... Rh8 +! 7 Kg3 Ke5 8 Ra6 Rh1 and White can make no headway. Also 6 ... Kf4 7 Ra4 + Kf3! still draws. Quite simple, but ...

| 6 ... | Ke5?? |

This loses the game.

| 7 Ra6! |

Now we can see the difference. White threatens 8 g5, and 7 ... Rh8 + 8 Kg5 Rg8 + would be followed by 9 Rg6 Rh8 10 Rg7 and 11 Kg6 with a win.

7 ...	Kf4
8 Rf6 +	Ke5
9 g5	

Larsen resigned, since his position is hopeless.

The other example is the following position from the Geller–Fischer game.

Geller–Fischer
Interzonal *1970*

Black to move

Despite the drawishness of the position, Fischer makes a last attempt to win.

1 ...   Rf1

Now 2 Kg3 Kg5 3 Kg2 leads to an easy draw. But Geller, exhausted by a long and difficult defense, blundered with ...

2 Rd2?

Black's reply, of course, was ...

2 ...   Kh4!

Now White's position looks desperate. Black threatens 3 ... g3, even after 3 Ke3. White can do nothing but take the pawn.

3 Kxf5   g3
4 f4   Kh3

Black still has problems to solve. As the actual continuation shows, this is not the way to improve his position. The immediate 4 . . . Ra1 would have saved a few moves.

5 Rd3!   Kh4

There is nothing better. If 5 . . . Kh2 White can achieve a draw with 6 Kg4! g2 (6 . . . *Rg1 7 f5*, etc.) 7 Rh3+ Kg1 8 f5 Kf2 9 Rh2!.

6 Rd2   Ra1

7 Ke5?

Although White's position looked desperate, only after this second mistake is it finally lost. A surprising draw was possible here by 7 Rd8!; e.g., 7 . . . g2 8 Rh8+ Kg3 9 Rg8+ Kf3 10 Ke6!! This astonishing move is the only way to save the game. Now 10 . . . g1Q 11 Rxg1 Rxg1 12 f5 Kg4 13 f6 draws easily; 10 . . . Ra4 is met by 11 Rxg2! Kxg2 12 f5 with a draw; and no improvement is offered by either 10 . . . Ra6+ 11 Ke7 Ra5 12 Ke6!! or 10 . . . Re1+ 11 Kd6.

By the way, White could have played Rd8 even earlier—for instance, instead of 6 Rd2. Then 6 Rd8 g2 7 Rh8 + Kg3 8 Rg8 + Kf3 9 Ke6! would have led to practically the same position. Even 5 Rd8 g2 6 Rh8 +, etc., was possible.

7 ...   Kg4!

This is the point. Now it's all over.

8 f5   Ra5 +
White resigned

This was another fine endgame from practical play that included hard-to-find points.

I hope these examples will convince everyone of the necessity of studying in detail even the simplest-looking endgames.

(*April 1971, September 1972*)

INDEX OF OPENINGS

Numbers refer to games.

JOIN THE U.S. CHESS FEDERATION

A special offer for readers of McKay chess books

Congratulations on your purchase of this fine McKay chess book. Now you can enjoy another competitive edge over other chess hobbyists by joining the more than 60,000 chessplayers who are members of the U.S. Chess Federation, the official chess organization in the U.S. since 1939.

As a U.S. Chess member, you'll receive a six-month subscription to *Chess Life*, the Federation's world-famous monthly magazine. You'll also receive other benefits—discounts on chess books and equipment, the opportunity to play in official tournaments (both across the board and through the mail)—and you'll get a national chess rating.

All of this at the special McKay reader's discount of just $9.95 for a full six months—that's more than a 33% discount off the regular membership price!

Say yes to U.S. Chess and we'll send you the FREE booklet "Ten Tips to Winning Chess" by International Grandmaster Arthur Bisguier.

Classic Titles from the McKay Chess Library

⌐	679-14108-1	**ART OF DEFENSE IN CHESS,** Andrew Soltis	$ 7.95
⌐	679-14101-4	**ART OF POSITIONAL PLAY,** Samuel Reshevsky	$ 9.95
⌐	679-14000-X	**ART OF SACRIFICE IN CHESS,** Rudolf Spielmann	$ 8.95
⌐	679-14002-6	**BASIC CHESS ENDINGS,** Reuben Fine	$14.95
⌐	679-14044-1	**CAPABLANCA'S 100 BEST GAMES OF CHESS,** H. Golombek	$ 8.95
⌐	679-14151-0	**CATALOG OF CHESS MISTAKES,** Andrew Soltis	$ 6.95
⌐	8129-1867-3	**CHESS FOR JUNIORS,** Robert Snyder	$13.00
⌐	679-14004-2	**CHESS FUNDAMENTALS,** J. R. Capablanca	$ 8.95
⌐	679-14005-0	**CHESS STRATEGY & TACTICS,** Fred Reinfeld	$ 6.95
⌐	679-14045-X	**DEVELOPMENT OF CHESS STYLE,** Dr. M. Euwe	$ 7.95
⌐	679-14109-X	**HOW TO PLAY GOOD OPENING MOVES,** Edmar Mednis	$ 6.95
⌐	679-14015-8	**HOW TO WIN IN CHESS ENDINGS,** I. A. Horowitz	$ 7.95
⌐	8129-1756-1	**IDEAS BEHIND THE CHESS OPENINGS,** Reuben Fine	$ 8.95
⌐	679-14325-4	**JUDGEMENT AND PLANNING IN CHESS,** Dr. M. Euwe	$ 6.95
⌐	8129-1923-8	**KARPOV-KASPAROV,** Don Maddox et al.	$15.00
⌐	679-14107-3	**KING POWER IN CHESS,** Edmar Mednis	$ 8.95
⌐	679-14403-X	**MAXIMS OF CHESS,** John W. Collins	$10.95
⌐	679-14021-2	**MIDDLE GAMES IN CHESS,** Reuben Fine	$10.95
⌐	8129-1785-5	**MODERN CHESS OPENINGS: New 13th Edition,** Walter Korn	$18.95
⌐	679-14103-0	**MODERN CHESS SACRIFICE,** Leonid Shamkovich	$10.95
⌐	679-14022-0	**MODERN CHESS STRATEGY,** Edward Lasker	$ 7.95
⌐	8129-1884-3	**NEW YORK TIMES CHESS BOOK OF GREAT CHESS VICTORIES AND DEFEATS,** Robert Byrne	$ 8.95
⌐	679-14154-5	**OFFICIAL RULES OF CHESS,** United States Chess Federation	$ 7.95
⌐	679-14475-7	**PAWN STRUCTURE CHESS,** Andrew Soltis	$ 8.95
⌐	679-14037-9	**WINNING CHESS TRAPS,** Irving Chernev	$ 8.95
⌐	8129-1866-5	**WINNING WITH CHESS PSYCHOLOGY,** Benko & Hochberg	$13.00

AVAILABLE IN BETTER BOOKSTORES OR SEE REVERSE SIDE
FOR ORDERING INSTRUCTIONS

Available from your local bookseller or

ORDER TOLL–FREE
1-800-733-3000

When ordering, please mention the following code:
005•07•POWER

OR SEND ORDERS TO:

RANDOM HOUSE, INC.
400 Hahn Road
Westminster, MD 21157
Attn.: Order Processing

—————— **Postage & Handling Rates** ——————

First Book $2.00
Each Additional Book...$0.50

Total from other side:

Number of books:_____ Total price: $_____

☐ Check or money order enclosed $ _____ (include postage and handling)

☐ Please charge $_____to my: ☐ MASTERCARD   ☐ VISA

Account No._____ Expiration Date_____
Signature _____

Name (please print) _____

Address_____ Apt. # _____

City_____ State_____ Zip _____